The Joe Lunchbucket Chronicles

The Joe Lunchbucket Chronicles

Tales and Travels
of an Aging Boomer

Outskirts Press, Inc.
Denver, Colorado

The Joe Lunchbucket Chronicles
Tales and Travels of an Aging Boomer
v2.0

Outskirts Press, Inc.
http://www.outskirtspress.com

ISBN: 978-1-4327-5744-1

Outskirts Press and the "OP" logo are trademarks belonging to Outskirts Press, Inc.

PRINTED IN THE UNITED STATES OF AMERICA

Dedication

These Chronicles are dedicated to Jane Lunchbucket (Babs), without her these stories may never have been completed. She has been at my side for over 40 years and has provided the support and inspiration I needed when the effort seemed to be more than I could muster. Her gentle encouragement of taking me out back and beating the tar out of me always seemed to bring back my drive to continue writing. She is an expert motivator and you can hardly see the bruises, bumps and scars. Seriously, Jane has been the love of my life, my partner and best friend. My hat (GOP) is off to her for being there and putting up with me for all these years.

I also dedicate these Chronicles to my two sons, Sean and Benjamin Lunchbucket, both of whom have been most helpful in reviewing the stories and adding artistic assistance. You two are the greatest!

And, I must add Cathy Colgrass-Edwards to this list. It was Cathy, through her relentless pursuit, who tracked us down and convinced us to attend the reunion that spawned the first story and then she pushed for more. Thank you for your support and encouragement, Cathy.

Table of Contents

Introduction

To Boomers One and All

Caution! Once you start down this path there may be no turning back. You will be compelled to reflect on those long summer days, your own rites of passage, that fair young maiden that twisted your heart into a pretzel, the boys of your youth that taunted, dared and lived the adventures at your side. What will you find? You will find good times. You will find sad times. You may find that the years have added perspective and made sense of many of the things you did. You will find that some of the things you did are still inexplicable. Are all of these issues covered in the Chronicles you hold in your hand? In some form or fashion yes; although some may still be trapped in our memories. Since there seems not to be a set chronology of memories and when they burst into the consciousness, maybe those that haven't shown up in this Chronicle will in a second or later volume; it is too early to tell.

Have you ever started a project that somehow took on a life of its own? Sure you have and so have I. Many months ago I attended a reunion of that old gang of mine. Many years had passed since I had seen or visited with any of them so I went to the gathering with some anxiety and a generous dose of curiosity. What would I find? Would I recognize and remember? Would I be recognized and remembered? What would the evening provide in the way of memories, good or ill? As it turned out it was a magical event and I felt compelled to write a brief story about the evening and the reminiscences shared that night through my own quirky perspective (*Reunion*). The story was shared with the group and was met with requests for more stories that might help us recapture (maybe re-live) those early days of <u>our</u> universe. What follows are a collection of stories that share those experiences.

Alas, shared experience is really a term subject to some interpretation, don't you think? After all, I would be spinning a whopper of a tale to think that everyone and anyone picking up the Chronicles had actually been there, in Brookfield, watching this unfold over the years beginning in the late 1950's and continuing through this very day. Yet somehow I think that maybe, just maybe, your stories may not be so far off the beaten path from that which Joe Lunchbucket has traveled. Maybe you will find yourself in these stories. Maybe these Chronicles will bring to mind memories of your own days of high adventure.

Joe Lunchbucket came to grips with the fact that neither he nor his experiences were unique unto themselves. What he discovered was that the collection of people, the times, events and places shared were unique. The Chronicles cannot just be stories to the reader; they need to be the gateway to your own remembrances. If you let yourself drift a little bit, stare off into space, you will soon find yourself, as Joe did, right back in the thick of it. You will find your own magical time and place. It's there waiting for you. Get going.

I would like to thank all of my friends, acquaintances and souls I have met along the way. Some of you were mentioned in the Chronicles; all were inspirational and consequential in the telling of these tales and travels. You have made it a walk more pleasant than I could ever imagine and I look forward to the memories that we have yet to create.

᠈᠈᠈

If you're like me when searching for something new to read, you may open a book or a web link so you might review a page or two in hopes that your review will help you make a decision whether to buy or keep looking. Well, here you are at that fork in your road; and you know what Yogi Berra once said..."*when you come to a fork in the road, take it.*" Now, how can you dispute that wisdom?

OK, I can't see the price tag on this literary masterpiece from where I sit; I don't know if you're paying retail, at a discount book outlet, a yard sale or thrift store. So, you are on your own making the expenditure decision. If you are considering buying these Chronicles retail, I know I will be glad you did and if you listen closely you can hear me cheering you on from the bunker where I write. Hey, it's not about the profit motive...well...OK it's a little about the profit motive...some ego and knowing I have touched a few lives and brought smiles to a few faces. Feel free to propel this Chronicle to the top of the New York Times Best Seller List...we'll both feel good about it.

Enjoy the Tales and Travels of an Aging Boomer!

CHAPTER **One**

"Reunion"

"And now the days grow short; we're in the autumn of our years; and we think of our lives as vintage wine from fine old kegs; from the brim to the dregs; it pours sweet and clear; it was a very good year"…or so the song composed by Ervin Drake would go, if we were to paraphrase it to define the personas of the beings that are the '8 Corners'.

The scrapbook of this assemblage of people who somehow came together nearly fifty years ago and who built lasting bonds to one another regardless of triumph or adversity belongs to Cathy Colgrass (Edwards). It is Cathy that has pieced this human mosaic together in the years after most childhood and young adult friendships turn to dust. It is she that has become the mortar that holds us together and brings us back in random years for the "**reunions**". This story is just a glimpse as seen through the eyes of the storyteller of the Sixth Reunion for those characters who ruled the 8 Corners.

We must first roll back the clock to the late 1950's and early 1960's. This time frame marks the "big bang" of the

8 Corners Group (henceforth, The Group; for lack of a more endearing moniker). In the embryonic stages there was a coming together of factional groups that in latter years would coalesce into one of the most amazing collections of diverse persons sharing <u>one</u> **magical lifetime experience**. I was fortunate to be one of those sojourners in this experience from the beginning.

Some of us had become friends before the beginning of the group. We shared the bonds of Cub Scouts, Girl Scouts, Little League, or elementary school classes and clubs. So the bond was already forming. The adhesion of the Group may be traced to two of the early places of congregation; the ice pond on Lincoln Avenue and just across the street at Simone's, the local penny candy store. Winters were spent skating at every chance. As winter turned to spring and summer, the lazy days were spent on a wooden soda case sitting out front of Simone's drinking Coke and munching penny pretzel sticks. In those days our modes of transportation were our feet and bicycles; we were all too young for cars yet. It was in these early days that the school and scout friendships were expanded to include others as Simone's quickly became THE place to meet. As the years passed the venue of the meeting place changed. The time for sitting on the soda case was drifting into history and sadly so was Simone's. However, ask any of the original Group and the memories of the candy shop on Lincoln Avenue will flood their minds with nostalgia and memories as sweet as the penny candy.

In my final year of elementary school, 1962, the new venue opened just across the street from Gross School. History may record that the first two of the Group to enter this establishment were Paul Malizzio and me. We would head to this new snack shop at the lunch break and again directly after school. We would play on the juke box the Booker T and the MG's tune *"Green Onions"* over and over again. It would not take long for word to spread that Steve and Grace's snack shop was the place to be. The Group would explode and the bonds we know today began.

Throughout the remainder of the early and middle 1960's, this was the official meeting place. Nothing, but nothing, happened without its root beginning at Steve and Grace's. After school, evenings and weekends we kept this place jumping; filling all the tables, counter and window ledges with bodies. Spending our bus and left over lunch money. It was here that the expansions of the Group really took root. Guys and gals from other schools besides RBHS and other towns adjacent to Brookfield started their pilgrimage to this Mecca. It was easy to find. It was just a half a block off the "8 Corners". The Group was birthed, the myth began to form and the legend was taking shape.

Life was good and we were enjoying the camaraderie. As one might expect, with the good times comes the bad. We lost a few of our friends to accidents and other…well, let's just say we lost them and they are missed, but this history is also a major factor in the solidarity of the Group. A shared loss builds a closeness that transcends the years.

Another issue was defending our turf. We had a great thing going and when that happens and the word spreads; then there will be others that want to take over that good thing for their own. We were a fun loving bunch, but we were not about to let some thugs from the city come in and change our model of community. Through the skirmishes the boys from Brookfield and those that were part of the Group from other towns defended the 8 Corners and our beauties in a fashion reminiscent of other historical battles…you know, like the Alamo or Iwo Jima. At long last, some were repelled, some moved on to conquer new realms and others found that the Group would assimilate them into the fabric that was us, if only they would ask and offer a hand of friendship.

During these years many things changed. Bicycles were discarded as we became of age to get our first passport to freedom…the driver's license. Now we had the family car, mobility and a sense of unlimited freedom. While we still socialized at Steve and Grace's and the occasional pick up softball game would occupy our time a new phenomenon was taking place. Boys were noticing girls and vice versa. The rite of passage was upon us and many of the great love stories began to unfold. Happily, there are many that endure to this day. Wow, that is a testimony to the bonds developed if ever there was one. Unfortunately, some of the matches we thought were made in Heaven worked out about as well as the 1962 Mets; unsalvageable.

Cars were not the only change. Fashion became an important factor of everyday life. This was more difficult than one might imagine. Why you might ask? Simple, there were two factions at RB (and I suspect at most other schools) the Cliques and the Greasers (anyone see the movie Grease?). Two different modes of dress were the distinguishing features. Cliques were the Madras shirt, Chino Pants and brown loafer fashion statement; and, Greasers were the Ban-Lon shirt, 7 Day Weekly pants and Gop (straw fedora for those that aren't from around here) attire. The young maidens did not seem to have this overriding fashion dissimilarity; their fashion was interchangeable with, perhaps, the exception of color. Greaser babes were much more likely to dress in darker colors with more ornate accessories and big hair, while the Clique maidens made a statement in pastel and a softer look…something akin to Gidget goes to camp. The bottom line here is which group you were affiliated with and what fashion statement needed to be made depended on the object of your affections, Grease or Clique. On the whole, the Group was Greaser. So the majority of your wardrobe was chosen for status among that faction. However, with mobility came anonymity and a transcending of factional lines. Some of the wardrobe budget had to be expended on and for the opportunity for crossover. Just don't get caught wearing brown loafers with weeklies! But all of this is for another chapter of my ongoing chronicles. Let's move back to the developing Group.

All these clothes and cars required money; money that was not supplied by mowing a few lawns. Real jobs were required. Even this did not cast the Group to the four directions in total. Sure, many took jobs here and there and remained with the Group, but en masse a good slice of the core group went to work at the Zayre Store in Forest Park. The Group infiltrated this retail outlet to an extent that it was like moving the Group from Steve and Grace's to the Zayre store. Are we beginning to get the picture of the remarkable continuity of this assemblage of persons? I would suggest that by this time this Group could not be separated with a nuclear explosion.

As the 1960's wound down and many were graduated from or graduating high school there was more change in the offing. Many of us were leaving the Group, at least temporarily. Some went on to college. Some went directly to work. The young men were caught in a terrible time. Viet Nam. This war took some of our friends and took from our friends the unlimited vistas that had lain before them. It was our good fortune that we lost just a few (it is still too many). Even these events did not completely splinter the Group. To be sure many, including myself, never returned to live, work and play in Brookfield, but after over a decade of shared laughs and tears, good and bad, love and breakup there was absolutely no way that any of us would ever NOT be part of this Group, this myth, this legend.

Over the passing years those that have remained in the vicinity of the 8 Corners have maintained friendships and contact, at least to some extent. For those of us that have moved on to other destinations there has always been… Cathy. And Cathy has always been synonymous with the REUNIONS. Correction, Cathy has always **been** the reunions. There have been 6 at this writing. We attended one in 1983 or 84 if memory serves and then lost touch. Through her relentless pursuit, Cathy managed to track us down for the reunion in 2006. A distant and expensive trip gave us ample reason to say thanks for thinking of us, but we cannot manage it; maybe next time. A few emails went back and forth and then Cathy asked that I call her. I did and she shared with me the list of those that would never again be sharing at our gatherings. That was the pivotal point that needed to be made to convince us to come to Brookfield. We committed and that brings us full circle by way of this twenty five cent tour.

We were seeing people that we had not seen in over 20 years; in some cases longer. For example, I had a conversation with Joe Buscemi and he asked me how long it had been since we last saw each other. It had been over four decades, and there we were catching up like it was only yesterday. One cannot imagine the joy we felt after all these years to see so many of our old, dear friends. It had been too long.

What I have attempted to put on paper here is a glimpse of what had started so many years ago. Through good fortune and persistence it has been kept as a living memory that comes together every few years and takes on a personal form. As we look at the photos that are taken at these reunions we see that the years have taken their inevitable toll. Some of us are a few grams overweight, some of the guys have grown too tall for their hair, many have a shade of hair color that denotes wisdom; wisdom that comes from living life and storing memories. When we all come together for these reunions though those photos become our future and we all revert to who we were back at the beginning, back in the 1960's; young and with the world out in front of us. It's...**magic**...and the way it should be for those who have shared that <u>one</u> **magical lifetime experience!**

To be continued...

CHAPTER **TWO**

Gops, Ban-Lon and Weeklies

Drift with me back to the late 1950's and consider the fashion statements we made as newly anointed teenagers or pre-teens. There were, of course, the denims, be these Levis, Wranglers or store brands. Jeans were always standard faire, although at some point in time they disappeared only to make a return in our early adulthood. Mid to late fifties brought us "Ivy League" slacks, you remember those with the tiny little buckles in the back; Calypso pants, these were calf length apparel for boys usually with some sort of rope belt, sort of a petal pusher for males…good grief, how pathetic…; boat neck shirts, and the emergence of button down collars (these stayed the course as uniform wear for the "non-greaser" throughout high school. Hey wait a minute…still). In short, we were all over the fashion map. Some might say off the edge of that map in retrospect. But just over the horizon was the defining moment for the majority of us as the decade turned and we began to assert our rightful place as precursors to the GQ man.

It is difficult to say if the fashion world was turned upside down by the apparel choices we began to make for the next several years. As the sixties progressed the duds our parents chose for us to keep us presentable gave way to a new look that, at this writing, passes reasonable understanding in our look back. However, there is no discounting the fact that we were the epitome of fashion, legends in our own mind!

The image created may have no equal before or since. The purveyors of this new look were not found at Nordstrom's, Saks Fifth Avenue or Bloomingdale's. Assembling this "Fab Ensemb" required diligent effort and travel into the belly of the city. What are we talking about here? Well, of course, the dawning of the age of **Gops, Ban-Lon** and **Weeklies!** A fashion craze that was destined to not take the world, continent, region, state or maybe even the near west side by storm.

OK, here is the game plan for seeking out the various accoutrements of this ensemble of choice (as short lived as it was in our history):

Gops, for those of you who have mercifully forgotten this era in the history of the 8 Corners, were hats, more appropriately, fedoras. Spring and summer wear dictated a straw variety, while fall and winter the sturdier felt. This head wear could be found at most local haberdasheries. A good choice for the gentlemen of the 8 Corners was Smith's Menswear in LaGrange. Smith's always carried an ample line of headwear for the discriminating greaser. There was a fashion tip to the wearing of the "gop". The brim had to be creased in just the right manner to project the total image for the overall aura being created. This meant that just the rearmost part of the brim was to be creased upward and the remaining brim downward. A word picture somehow does not do it justice, so dig deep and remember the vivid picture that is emblazoned in the recesses of your mind. Got it? Let's move on then to the next item; Ban-Lon.

Ban-Lon, while a fabric of some unknown chemical concoction, was the preferred fabric of the shirts worn with the gop. Long sleeve, short sleeve, buttons down the full front or just a three button pull over, the choices seemed endless. Colors were usually muted in grays, greens, and blues with the required blacks and whites. Never would you find, or if you did be caught dead in one, a brightly colored or "aloha" festooned Ban-Lon shirt. This article of the uniform of the day was a little more difficult to find. Oh for sure, there were Ban-Lon wannabes available in local stores, but to get the real stuff required a train trip, usually on a day when we were conspicuously absent from class-es, to the fashion Mecca known as Maxwell Street. Here one found the mother lode of desirable Ban-Lon shirts. Nirvana! The ladies reading this are at this point beside themselves, breaking into a sweat and breathing heavily just thinking of the Beau Brummell look we are recreating here. Control yourselves fair maidens we're not done yet. We must put some trousers on these avant garde gods of fashion! Enter the Weeklies.

Weeklies nearly round out the fashion statement. The trousers of choice could be found in the work clothes sec-tion at any discriminating Sears store on the planet. The total look was to be found in a variety of colors available (gray, green or blue) and the length. While any reputable tailor will advise that the trousers break at shoe top, it was understood by the fashion moguls of the 8 Corners that the cuffed Weeklies stopped a good 4 inches above the shoe top! (Perhaps, we never psychologically recovered from the trauma of Calypso pants). Thus, the purchase was to be made buying the correct waist size, but a length for someone several inches shorter than the ultimate wearer. I know I'm starting to hallucinate with this trip down memory lane.

Finally, we reach the footwear required to complete the look. Without question black socks were required. Could you even imagine this get up with a pair of Argyles? Or white? Good Lord have you no sense of fashion at all? The shoes required, also black, left no room for loafers...most especially penny loafers...but required a tie shoe, elevated heel, moderately pointed toe, smooth leather brought to a high shine; wingtips in any variety need not apply. And, there you have it. Head to toe the Renaissance man inhabiting the 8 Corners circa 1962-64.

Oh what a glorious vision we projected! Can you see it in your mind's eye back those many years? Admit it we were ahead of our time. If it weren't for us, Versace and Armani would have been ordinary; they would have had no model to build on. Am I too over the top with that one? Maybe. But, you have to admit the early GQ man of the 8 Corners was destined to become...the man, the myth the legend!

Thankfully, fashions come and go and to our good fortune rapidly. As I scribe this, another chapter of the "**Joe Lunchbucket Chronicles**", I can still see my entire former cohort laughing, living and running headlong through life dressed as they were in Gops, Ban-Lon and Weeklies. Let us never forget the fact and lore that has made us who we were and who we have become.

CHAPTER **Three**

The Memory is in the Music

Just the other night I was surfing the channels and found a program on PBS that not only brought a smile to my face, but a flood of memories so rich that it was almost as if I had been transported back in time. The program did exactly what it was designed to do and that is to get all of us "boomers" to reflect fondly on and recapture our youth for 90 minutes, and open our wallets to support PBS.

Hey, we have all been on this journey since the late 50's together in some form or fashion, so admit it...you too have stopped on your tip-toe through the cable offerings and were compelled to come to a screeching halt when those melodious tones of the "Doo Wops" filled your living room. You, like me, stopped to listen to just that one memorable song being performed at that moment, because it reminded you of an event, a summer, or the Hubba Hubba du jour. Also, like me, 90 minutes later you were audibly singing along to some really great tunes and remembering so many things, thoughts, joys, sadness, and most of all, those you shared these times with those many years ago.

As the program progressed, I began visualizing the experiences that surrounded the particular tune being performed. An hour into the program the host introduced Kathy Young and the Innocents. I did not recognize the name, but after a few notes I did recognize the song; "A Thousand Stars in the Sky". It was instant transport back to the gymnasium at Gross School and "Top Graders", the Friday night sock hop for 7th and 8th graders. These weekly gatherings provided an opportunity for the young ladies to practice being "oh, so coy" so they could hone their skills, which became considerable I might add, for making the young men feel totally unworthy of their attention. Of course, for us young men the opportunity presented us with a venue to test drive our raging hormones! This explosive combination rivaled anything that could have been concocted in the chemistry lab. Unfortunately, the end result was the girls dancing together and the guys practicing looking cool or tough against the wall or in the bleachers. The sock hop would end, the coyness, now taken to a higher level, secured until next week and the hormones, exhausted, would have to wait another seven days for the ritual to start all over again. I would bet that for most of us this was the introduction to the "8 Corners" tribal dance ritual.

Leaving the sock hop behind we were feeling pretty cocky after finally signing up for Fortnightly...aka, dance lessons (now there's a dusty memory). Now we could actually go to a dance for the main attraction...dancing; impress the girls with our Fred Astaire like footwork, and, without question, take the raging hormones out for another test drive. We were ratcheting it up a level and moving on to the local Saturday dances with live bands. Attending these dances was a rite of passage. The preparation was like choreographing _West Side Story_. The maidens were beguiling in their very best attract-the-raging-hormone outfit. The young studs were decked out in the very latest fashionable suit from Sears or Penney's (this was pre-historic times for GQ), tab collar shirts and pencil thin ties. Shoes were sporting a high shine and we were out the door like the US Postal Service; rain, sleet or dark of night would not keep us from our appointment with destiny. Thank God these dances were local. Why you might ask? The answer is that none of us were of driving age. Have any of us ever really contemplated how pathetic we must have been, going through this Kabuki never giving a thought to the fact that we had just recently been released from selling GS cookies door to door or working on turning our Bobcat pin right side up? Contemplations like these sort of make you shiver, real sudden like.

But I digress. Let us take stock of where these soirées took place. The standard bearers were St. Barbara's, SOKOL Hall, VFW, Moose and St. Louise. Since attendance was dependent on foot traffic, cotillions outside of this area were out of the question...for now.

Music ceased being provided by phonograph and was replaced by some of the best local bands available. Take a trip back in time and remember: The Fabulous Imperials (thank you Cliff, Bob, Al and Jimmy); The Maybees and The Jesters. The music they played was sensational. The beat was mesmerizing. The girls, with finely honed skills by this time, were still administering crushing defeats to the pent up raging hormones. (Well, some things morph more slowly than others.) As we meander down our time line even these local dances began to pale as we expanded our horizons to other venues. High school opened new vistas and our journey found us at Youth Center in Riverside, dances at churches and fraternal halls in Berwyn, North Riverside and other close by suburbs. We were getting mobile and taking advantage of this as if there were no tomorrow.

I must insert a Joe Lunchbucket note here. I have to admit I am reliving the memory even as I write this ode to our early years. It is amazing what a CD of 60's music can do for poking the ant hill of my memory. What does *"Sugar Shack"* bring to mind? Or maybe that old favorite from our very own 8 Corners Hymnal, immortalized by who other than the Kingsmen..."*Louie Louie*"! Indulge yourself, it's not too late.

As life unfolds we discover that permanence is not permanent. The bands we so dearly loved splintered, moved on to other locales or reformed into new groups. Some of our own went on to some fame and fortune. Even your raconteur gained some notoriety as a balladeer. Of course, I speak of the all most famous, semi-legendary band of renown know to one and all far and wide as the Sultans! (OK I'm over the top on that, but just a tad). What we lacked in musical skill we made up for in showmanship and connection with the audience. Of course, it helped that our audience was all of you staring in and reading this chronicle! We did have the time of our life playing in all sorts of places with a variety of crowds who all seemed to enjoy the show. Let's have a show of hands for all out there who remember weekends spent at the Red Bench in Downers Grove.

There remains for me one band related memory that stands high above the rest. The Sultans were a fixture at the Bench, playing there most every weekend for months.

When the management decided to hold a battle of the bands, we were certainly favored to win it all. After our performance, I too was certain of it. The competition of other local bands just didn't measure up. Even WLS radio sent a band named Clark Weber's Cobras; sorry, but they were as exciting as watching paint dry. The Sultans were polishing up our acceptance speeches for awards night with one week to go; victory was in the bag. On the last week of the competition I decided to go and personally review the last band to compete. By the end of the night I was looking for a match to set my award winning acceptance diatribe aflame. The band that played that night was from another planet I was sure. It had the usual faire, guitars, drums, bass, singing. What was new and sensational was the horn section. I was depressed.

Truth be told, I suspected that this band would be something special. The drummer who had put this group together was just back from a national tour; his beat was as spectacular as always. It was a special revue and I would have expected noting less. This was not the first time that I had enjoyed his music, but Jimmy Beck and his All-Stars were more than even I could have anticipated. Hell, given the opportunity I would have voted for his band to win. OK enough pain…we still love you Jimmy!

To quote Bob Dylan, "the times they were a changing"; some of us were going off to college, some to serve their country, others getting married and this was impacting the cohesive group attendance at these outings. Oh, there were still more dances to be danced at places like Cheetah, and the Purple Twig, but the innocence of Top Graders, St Barb's and other local dances was disappearing rapidly in our rear view mirror. There is no need to

mourn the disappearance, we all must grow and progress and, inevitably age. If we did not, then there would
be nothing to wax nostalgic about. And, if we could not
do that, how then would we recapture our youth through
those fond and glorious melodies and memories.

Today our group has it's own Jeff Agonath to keep the
memories as fresh as the morning dew with his disk jock-
eying and, apparently, a Las Vegas revue featuring himself
as Bobby Darrin! I vote for Jeff being the star at our next
reunion. I for one would love to hear him croon "Beyond
the Sea", "Mack the Knife" and "Splish Splash". Query:
will his lovely spouse Bev co-star as Sandra Dee?

There it is then, laid out before you. All you need do is
focus when those tunes come on the radio, or PBS. Let your
mind drift back and you will find yourself subconsciously
reliving those days of yesteryear as if you were right there,
right then. Take your own walk down memory lane; and you
will find yourself "Under the Boardwalk", "On Broadway",
in a "Town Without Pity", thinking "He's So Fine", or about
a "Long Cool Woman (In A Black Dress)"; all you have to
do is listen, close your eyes, be a "Wanderer" and think
back. **The memory is in the music!**

CHAPTER **Four**

"Haute Cuisine"

American Astronauts are in constant communication with Mission Control at the LBJ Space Center near Houston. Who will forget those frightening words from Apollo 13; "Houston we have a problem." It was Mission Control where our celestial missions began; it was Mission Control from where planning and execution of the flights were managed; it was Mission Control where problems were solved; yes, Mission Control was the nerve center of our manned space flight. Successful coordinated efforts require a central command post.

By now, you are scratching your head and wondering what has the American Space Program to do with "haute cuisine"? Simply, the answer is nothing, but it is a great attention getter and to note that our "Group" also had a mission control and that final nerve center (at least for Joe Lunchbucket) was Manley's, the diner/deli right at the heart of Brookfield on the 8 Corners. This was the gathering point for the evening's activities and the hub where planning our assaults on the weekend took shape. Our missions all began at Manley's. Manley's deli was part of our very own brand of "haute cuisine". Was the food served there exotic, pretentious or prepared by high-toned chefs of renown? In a word, no they were not. Most, if not all, of the faire was prepared by Manley and/or his folks. Was it the dining experience that you would note in the same sentence with "Tavern on the Green", the "Brown Derby" or "Ruth's Chris Steak House? Again, the answer would be no. They did make some terrific sandwiches, burgers and desserts and without question some of the tastiest fruit filled dumplings anywhere! Other than prom night, weddings or family outings, this was our "haute cuisine" back in the day. It too was our mission control... Manley, we have a problem! And, like any good mission director Manley would answer the call and help solve that problem. You see, haute cuisine requires more than just the fine food, it requires the entire package of food, ambiance, location and the human element and Manley's had it all for us at that time of our lives.

But alas it did not all start at Manley's; there were predecessors. It is time to relax and travel back to an earlier time in our lives. A time to visit some of the other eateries (using the term loosely on occasion) that served as our mission control du jour.

As the 8 Corners Group was beginning to take shape there were several places that presented themselves as fine eateries; especially when we were pre-teens. Beginning with penny candy at Marie's directly across from Gross School on Broadway. This was the place to go for the essentials in food; colored candy stuck to long sheets of paper, waxed tubes or bottle shapes containing some color and flavor of sugar water, the ever popular Bulls-eye candies, jelly beans and pretzel rods. Not exactly the most nutritious menu, but hey, we were children with underdeveloped palates.

Another favorite haunt at these earlier ages required a long trek to downtown Brookfield and Paden's drug store (later to become the Purple Plum restaurant). This was the quintessential drug store with, perhaps, the last of the "real" soda fountains. I do not recall eating at Paden's, unless ice cream has become one of the major food groups, but for a fountain drink this was THE place to go. Old Man Paden would personally squirt just the right amount of soda syrup (flavored to your choice) and hand-mix your cool drink with the seltzer water right from the tap at the fountain. I can still see him adding the seltzer while twirling the long spoon to mix the soda flavor into the coke or root beer of a lifetime. Here, before the soda companies caught up, was the beginning of the cherry coke, vanilla coke and…a drum roll please…the Boogie Beer (pronounced Boo-Gee). Boogie Beer was a Paden's original hand mixed root beer with a squirt of chocolate. I'm feeling faint. We must move on.

While in the geographic vicinity we should mention Fisher's Pharmacy across the street. Fisher's too had a soda fountain, but it was more of a lunch counter and did not have the credentials of a real soda fountain like Paden's. What it did sport was the mission control for a few of our dear friends; in particular Cliff St. John. Some of my earliest memories of Cliff were of him securing his spot on the last two stools at the counter where he consumed a large amount of coffee and, sort of, held court. Cliff was the man! He had the demeanor, the look and the Cheetah sweater that would secure his place as a god among us. If they are not, those two stools should be in the Smithsonian!

Of course a short meander over the tracks took us to the ice cream Mecca of Prince Castle (changed to Cock Robin for some unknown reason years later). If it was an ice cream sundae that you desired, there was no better place than Prince Castle and the Top Hat Sundae. I am not sure if it was the ice cream or the square scoops that made this a stop on the haute cuisine trail of our youth. Of course, the Brook Park contingent would argue that the frozen custard at Kerry's on Maple and 31st was better faire. In my considered opinion it is too close to call; living in the middle I frequented both.

Like the Cosmos coalescing into form, the 8 Corners Group began to take shape at what might be the first Mission Control…Simone's. Candy store, hobby shop and general hang out; Simone's was to Brookfield what Doc's was to the Jets in West Side Story. We did not have tables and chairs or even a counter. What we had were empty wooden soda crates that worked well for makeshift seating around the pot belly stove during the winter or lounge chairs out front during the heat of the summer. This served us well for a number of years and during that time all activity began, day or night, at Simone's. The cuisine you ask? Cokes, bags of Jay's BBQ chips, pretzel rods, Mallow Pies, Reese's Peanut Butter Cups and more Cokes. Surely enough sugar to hype us up for decades to come. This was not Attention Deficit Disorder; this was a prolonged sugar buzz.

In 1962, Steve and Grace opened the snack shop across the street from Gross School. This, I submit, was the "big bang" of the 8 Corners Group. By this time we were all in high school or rapidly approaching this rite of passage. Regardless, Steve & Grace's Snack Shop served as our new hub for all activity. The days of the penny candy and sitting on soda crates faded into oblivion and so eventually did Simone's; although it should be on the list of historical landmarks. In years previous to the opening by Steve and Grace, this very spot was the site of a chicken take out food service named Kwik Chick. That name stuck and we used it interchangeably for Steve & Grace's Snack Shop. Our menu graduated to fries drowned in ketchup, greasy burgers and, of course, Coke. We all could have been poster boys and girls for Tums and Clearasil. Alas, the menu was secondary. Kwik Chick was the center of the universe. It represented our base of operation, our dugout for the softball games played in the school yard, our sanctuary and the precursor to the singles bar. I am quite certain we each fell in love repeatedly at Kwik Chick, so even dating emanated from this central control station.

As we gained mobility with the family car or our own first beater we branched out to other eateries. After dances at St. Barb's, SOKOL or VFW it might be Ralph's in downtown Brookfield, Rocky's north of 31st (before it became Barone's) or maybe Sonny's on Ogden. Kwik Chick was not a late night establishment, so after the initial rendezvous the course of the evening would branch out to A&W, Tops and other drive-in restaurants where we could (if one was fortunate enough to have one) show off our muscle cars. The cuisine changed very little among these stops. The usual burger, fries, soda or shake were pretty standard; of course, root beer and a dog at A&W. About this time two new cuisines of note came on our RADAR; Carm's on Roosevelt Road near Harlem and Novi's on Oak Park and Ogden. Without question two of the premier Italian Beef eateries in the Chicago area. To this day the argument continues about which has the best offering. I'll leave it at that.

This brings to mind a humorous tale. The bachelor party for Ray Svihlik was a controlled drunk out. At the time, yours truly, Joe Lunchbucket, was racing his now semi-legendary, almost famous MOPAR, **Dr. Go,** sponsored by Earl Wheeler's SUNOCO station in North Riverside. As marathon beer drinking normally does, it soon turned into a serious need for food, good food, hot food...red meat! What better way to subdue the hunger of house-ful of underage drunken loons? Why Novi's Italian beef sandwiches without question! Earl and I elected to make the big beef run. All systems were go on the Doctor and we drove all the way from Larry LaJeone's house to Novi's in Berwyn, surely at close to the speed of light. Believe me in our condition even NASA would have marveled at our command of telemetry and the retro-burns needed to ne-gotiate the winding ways of Riverside and the high-speed traffic on Ogden. Novi's was still housed in the converted gas station at the time and the skill needed to enter the overcrowded parking lot qualified Earl for LUNAR Landing Module command. Joe Lunchbucket was near blackout by this time...must have been the G's we pulled in our record run to Novi's. Earl and I walked, no wait, stumbled into Novi's and were in the back of an extremely long line be-ing pressed up against the wall and generally getting pretty feisty and irritated. We were there for meat and plenty of it. We were bullet proof and truly feeling MOTU status. We were in no mood or condition to be kept waiting, so when the call came for who's next, we both screamed out **we want 40 beefs!** Well that certainly got their atten-tion and moved us to the front of the line post haste. We bludgeoned our way to the front of the line and up to the counter and rounded out our order with 1 small fries and 2 small Cokes. Grabbing our ginormous order of beef we made the return flight to LaJeone's to feed the drunken horde. When it absolutely has to get there on time...call Earl, Joe and Dr Go...eat your heart out FedEx! (Note: Just in case you are acronym intolerant, MOTU is Master of the Universe...a condition manifest after an evening of drinking beer as if it was soon to be prohibition.).

Forgive my digression into the tales of the unwashed. Moving along to other eateries of note from the early days we have arrived at the perfunctory dateless night and late night ports of call.

Let's have a show of hands out there. Does anyone at all except Denny Davidson and I remember Walt's Cellar Inn? Kenny Basco I know you can own up to it and I am sure there are a few others. Walt's Cellar Inn was a bar in the basement of Walt's (last name unknown) home somewhere in south Brookfield. The motif of this fine pub was under-age only. A great place to wile away the hours on those dateless nights and/or after the femme fatale of the day was returned to her parents. I don't recall ever seeing a female at Walt's. This was strictly a mano y mano hideaway for serious drinking and low stakes poker. Other than pretzels or the occasional delivered pizza it was strictly a liquid diet. The most amazing story to come out of Walt's is the evening Denny and I hatched the idea to do something really out of the ordinary...the next day we began our lost weekend in New York. Actually it was just a high priced extension of Walt's with great live jazz music.

The final stop for late, late, late...OK go to bed you SOB... was Red's on Ogden and Maple. This truly was the last stop in more ways than one. Cuisine? Breakfast, and that menu is pretty hard to screw up and we would have been incapable of noticing anyway. If this were a movie, we would fade to black.

This would take us full circle and the next day or evening it would all start again at either Kwik Chick or Manley's. I titled this "haute cuisine" and really thought I might do a more culinary expose, but as I got into this I realized that it was the places and not the cuisine that was truly important. It was in these places that we shared our lives and to some extent our hopes and dreams through unending conversations. It was also another building block in the lasting structure of the 8 Corners legend.

One can hope that these words have brought back memories and reminded you of the follies of our youth. I know Joe Lunchbucket is smiling!

CHAPTER

Let the Games Begin

It wasn't an ordinary place. It was a magical place. My earliest recollections are of a landscape that was wrought with danger; especially for a young lad just starting Kindergarten and on to the early years of school. There were swing sets with strap seats, not the hard straight seats like at home in the backyard. There was a climbing station, referred to as "monkey bars" that offered all sorts of potential perils and hazards. There was a slide so tall that I'm sure there were clouds around the pinnacle of the ladder that I had to climb to get to the slide. It was akin to Sir Edmund Hilary's ascent of Everest. But the scariest part was the ground itself. Back then, the ground was not a hard asphalt surface (which is treacherous enough for young boys and girls) as it is now. Back then, it was a playground covered in cinders. Old burnt coal offerings that had the consistency of a diamond and the edge of a finely honed razor. Good grief, a kid could go to recess and one false move could render him as film footage for the most despicable slasher film. It's a wonder we survived or, at least, survived with all our limbs attached. In today's world that surface and those playground accessories would be fodder for a mammoth lawsuit waiting to happen. Somehow we did survive, played, ran, fell, cried, got repaired and did it all over again. We even mastered scaling the slide so high there were oxygen tanks at the top.

At age five or six this playground was the modern day equivalent of the Obstacle/Confidence Course found at any US Army Basic Training facility. No, we weren't in training for the Airborne Ranger Division of the Cub Scouts; this was recess and the commando course was the Gross School playground.

Over the years the playground landscape changed. The cinders gave way to smooth asphalt, so falls now produced mere scraps instead of lacerations requiring trauma units. The playground equipment stayed, but as we grew older it was abandoned to the new tikes and we moved up to other levels of competitive games.

In third or fourth grade there wasn't even a hint of talk about global warming; at least, not on the playground. The winters during those years were typical...snow that was butt deep to a tall giraffe. When this winter cycle arrived some of us opted to stay at school during the lunch break; opting to brown bag rather than hoof it home as was the normal routine at Gross School. Our goal was not to avoid the cold weather and snow, nor was it to get in a few additional minutes of homework time. It was to gain access to the playground, butt deep to a tall giraffe in snow, without the throngs of children for a good forty-five minutes of full contact tackle pom-pom. This should be an Olympic competition with the three medals going to the last three standing. The basics of this game were simple. All players would line up against the building wall. The "would be tackler" would position themselves in the middle of the playground. Safety lay at the other side of the playground along the fence on Broadway. On the signal of the tackler it was a mad dash for the fence. Someone would get tackled and now there were two in the middle. This would continue back and forth until there was but one runner and a gazillion tacklers. Obviously, the last one standing, not tackled, was the winner, but still he or she would run the gauntlet until found face first in the snow with a gazillion small sweaty bodies piled on top. I'm pretty certain in latter years this became the screen play for Arnold's Sci-Fi thriller "Running Man". Now I don't want to brag, but Joe Lunchbucket was quite fleet of foot back in the day and had all the moves of a healthy Gale Sayers, so avoiding tackles was a walk in the park...until. Until the most dreaded tackler of all was in the middle ground waiting to pounce on the next victim, taking them to the snow covered school yard with all the finesse of Dick Butkus. Some bruiser of a third or fourth grader is what you are thinking right now. Well, you would be wrong. This kid was quick, agile and when focused on the target was as deadly as a combat pilot getting missile lock.

Don't make eye contact. Use some other unsuspecting kid as your human shield. Run for the fence or wall taking the most direct, but distant route possible from this warrior. Many a time, as fleet as I may have been, was I caught and taken down by this nemesis of the Gross School Tackle Pom-Pom Winter Games. Bob, weave, change direction completely, vary speed, shadow some other runner...it made no difference you were dead meat and would soon be spread eagle face down eating snow. A true gladiator and champion and one to be enshrined in the Tackle Pom-Pom Hall of Fame; that's how I remember Peggy Kosik in those early years. We remained friends throughout elementary and high school, and although I have not seen her in many years, rumor has it that on a cold and snowy winter day, when the snow is butt deep to a tall giraffe, on the Gross School playground the ghosts of tackle pom-pom past can still be seen in an eerie fog and Peggy is taking down another fleet of foot runner.

The schoolyard hosted many other games over the years. In the spring, the schoolyard would come alive with softball games. The school had painted yellow bases and base paths on the asphalt to accommodate our own boys of summer. Still in the middle years at Gross School I remember watching intently the 8th graders play softball; they were the kings and rulers of the schoolyard. The names have faded into memories lost, but the sight of the games is still fresh. Good lord, those boys could hit that sixteen inch softball a mile. As I grew up we continued the softball in that schoolyard all the way through our high school years. On the weekends we would all meet at Steve & Grace's and soon the game would begin...sometimes the end was long in coming. I'm not sure, but I think I'm close on this one, when I say 20 innings of softball was about the norm. There were some stellar players too. Little Joe Smith was an outfielder to be reckoned with, because he was too tall to get the ball over his head. Blast one out his way and he would start running back on it, stick up one of those long gangly arms and he would snag it in one of his routine circus catches. Denny Graber was another outfielder of legend. Not for circus catches, but because of his throwing ability. I have never seen anyone who could throw a softball from the wall of Tlapa's Grocery to home plate on Broadway with the ball never going above or below 3 feet off the ground at what looked, sounded and felt like the speed of sound. Simply unbelievable! Our problem was finding someone, anyone, with the courage to catch it. At best, you would have to sacrifice your body for the good of the team and just stop it. How we enjoyed those games.

In grade school we created another baseball game designed for three players. We would draw a box with an X from corner to corner and a circle in the middle on the wall of Gross School. This was the strike zone. The batter would stand facing Broadway. There would be a pitcher and an out fielder. Our equipment was regular wooden bats (aluminum bats were not invented yet), standard baseball gloves and a $.49 rubber baseball. Three outs and positions were rotated. Outs were recorded with strike outs or fly outs; anything else was a single to facilitate keeping some semblance of a score. Hey, somebody had to win otherwise what was the purpose? Unlike today, we had no trouble having winners and losers in a game; we had no tender ego that might get bruised and turn us into an axe murderer in later life. This game, unlike the 20 innings of softball, could go on indefinitely, or until somebody just gave out in exhaustion. Then it was off to Marie's or Simone's for a Coke and one of the major food groups… Hershey, Jay's or Hostess; you know…power food! There were regulars that would pick up this game at a moment's notice. Ken and Dave Arndt, John Cameron, Ricky Keslov. Mike Tomillo and, of course, Joe Lunchbucket to name a few seemed to always be ready to engage in this precursor of home run derby. During the spring and summer months our gloves were always close at hand or attached to the handle bars of our bikes. All we needed was a bat and Ken, Dave, Ricky and Mike all lived very close to Gross School, so bats were always at the ready too. You have to appreciate the inventiveness of the young mind in finding ways to entertain and pass the time on our long summer days.

It would be an understatement to say that the Gross School playground was an integral part of our maturing process. The games at all ages brought us together, bonded friendships, made us laugh...and cry...and provided memories that are as endearing today as the competition was back then. We're at the age that baseball and softball are something to be watched more that being an active participant. As for an afternoon of tackle pom-pom on the schoolyard covered in snow butt deep to a tall giraffe... my money is still on Peggy.

CHAPTER **Six**

War Ponies and the Mystic Warriors

In the Native American cultures the men, the warriors, rode to fame on their great "war ponies". These fine animals would carry them to the hunt, the scout or the battle. When engaging in battle with other tribes or the US Cavalry it was customary to paint their war ponies, making them ready, as they readied themselves, for the battle to come. Just imagine the sight of a fine horse and rider painted to look as fierce as possible; it was surely formidable. One may contemplate that a percentage of any battle fought is determined by the look of the foe; a look that strikes fear in the opposition may surely tip the scales of victory.

In the lore of the 8 Corners there were many of our own contemporaries and acquaintances that were "mystic warriors" with their own war ponies. Some of the ponies were unassuming, others were painted to be extremely imposing; all were war ponies in their own right and their warriors all fierce competitors. Yours truly, Joe Lunchbucket, was certainly one of those "mystic warriors" and his war pony was indeed an imposing mount.

Our battles were fought on far west 31ˢᵗ Street, Ogden at Cicero Ave, County Line Road, Oswego, US 30 and Union Grove. These could have been the names of fierce battle engagement locations, but, of course, there were no battles with the US Cavalry and the battles we did engage in were always one on one and the contest a combination of skill, speed and most definitely…horsepower. Sit back, strap in and let your memory conjure up the sights, smells and sounds of sanctioned and street drag racing! As I write this I am picturing myself foot tuning my MOPAR with the tuned headers wide open, blasting that deep throated rumble of nearly 400 horsepower into an otherwise still and serene pastoral vision. Oh this is music to my ears!!!

Warriors and war ponies clashing at any given traffic light that provides multiple lanes and a straight-away is a right of passage. The sound of squealing tires and the smell of burning rubber on a warm summer evening signals that the battle has begun. These were usually just the prelude to our 'days of thunder'. If the jousting appeared to call into question the pride of either warrior or his war pony, then a parlay would take place to determine a suitable location for an all out quarter mile. Make no mistake, we would break the sound barrier if we had to any where a race would present itself; however, that said it was always better to remove that pesky traffic concern and find a suitable stretch of unimpeded highway to really let the horses run.

As I reflect on a few of those painted war ponies, several come instantly to mind. Sonny Stepul's Grim Reaper was the scourge of Berwyn, Lyons and many of the local drag strips. The Reaper was much modified, very fast and very imposing. Just the sight of that black 1964 Dodge painted with the Grim Reaper, scythe in hand, and sporting those twelve inch wrinkle wall slicks sent many a would be challenger whimpering away.

One imposing war pony appeared on the horizon and somehow one knew that this was a warrior and pony to be reckoned with. No war paint to speak of, just a simple name on the rear fender...Wooly Bully. This dark 1966 Dodge Coronet was nothing short of awesome. Powered by a 426 Hemi with two four barrel carburetors, when the headers on this beast were open the windows on my car rattled and I was a hundred feet away. One hot night the race of the summer was shaping up out on far west 31st Street. This Hemi powered denizen was set for a match race against the big block Corvette of Larry Mitch, owner of the SUNOCO station in Brookfield. There was a parade of muscle cars that went out to watch this clash of Titans in the dark of the evening. They lined up heading east on 31st right where 31st Street goes over Route 83. An impartial and very brave aficionado stood between these two powerful ponies flashlight in hand making sure the contest was a fair and clean start. The roar of the finely tuned engines was deafening even from a distance. There weren't many houses out there back in those days, but we all knew this would be a one shot race before the spoilers sporting badges showed up to curtail the thunder and any thought of a second or third tie breaker. These warriors knew that it was all out on the first run. A flick of the light to each driver and then a drop of the light and it all began; the horsepower was unleashed and the race was over before one could blink. They went from dead stop to a quarter mile finish in some 11 seconds. These two war ponies flew passed my vantage point well in excess of 100 mph! Predictably, the County Sheriff showed up on queue just minutes after the warriors faded into the distance. There was no chance of them being caught; they had vanished into the night. Larry Mitch won that battle. Legend has it that the Woolly Bully missed a critical power shift into third gear that cost him precious seconds. If they ever met again, perhaps the outcome may have been different. Some time later I met up with Wooly Bully at Oswego, he confirmed he missed that gear. I assure you he didn't miss any on that Sunday at Oswego.

We certainly had our local warriors and war ponies as well. One of my fondest memories was the feeling I had riding in what was to become the automobile of my dreams, a 1962 Corvette. Many a time was I given the privilege to ride home from RB or after church at St. Louise in that 'candy apple red' Corvette of George Hesik. I have never forgotten the power and style of that car. To this day I keep a scale model of a candy-apple red 1962 Corvette on my desk as a reminder. Yes folks, Joe Lunchbucket aspires to own a used car!

Does the Hobey Picker ring a bell with anyone? Picture the silver 1964 Chevelle all painted with the moniker and a giant mushroom on the side. This pony belonged to Frank Cermak; and while I am not sure what mushrooms had to do with muscle cars, Frank's pony did offer an interesting aesthetic.

Perhaps, the most remembered of the war ponies was one that was not noted for its speed. It was imposing, it did have a name and it was beloved by all of us at the 8 Corners. Who could forget the Sherman tank, remanufactured into an old Mercury, painted flat black and adorned with the moniker "Queste Bandito"? This machine was not built for speed or silent running…it was a beast and a automobile of legend!

I could go on indefinitely with the listing of muscle cars and wannabe muscle cars, but let's get to the roar of the lakes pipes!

One summer evening in 1966, we gathered at the home of Larry Spath for an impromptu backyard party. We were enjoying a little BBQ, soft drinks and watermelon. Larry thought it might be fun to have a water fight…you know squirt guns, water balloons, fire hoses…all the usual stuff. Soon the watermelon was put in play; perhaps, it started with the all important seed spitting contest, that turned into chunk tossing and from there it got ugly. One distinct memory of that fateful evening was Larry using Maddy Ziolkowski's head as a juicer for the end of the citrullus lanata. Larry just sort of sauntered over with the full end of a melon, jammed it on Maddy's head and proceeded to twist it back and forth melding the flesh of the melon into her long dark (now red and seeded) locks. Without question, Maddy was close to homicide. But I digress; the point of my chronicle is war ponies, not melon heads. It was at this very soirée that my mighty MOPAR donned its war paint for the very first time. Larry, twice in one evening, was struck with another capital idea…let's paint a name on the sides of my car. It was a Friday; Sunday was race day at Oswego so it all fell nicely into place. Larry just happened to have some paint on hand and he was a bit of an artistic sort, so at that very moment the legend was birthed. No longer was it just a 1966 Dodge Coronet 500 with a 383, 4-speed…garden variety muscle car…it was transformed before our very eyes into "Dr. GO"! That Sunday at Oswego Drag Raceway the Dr. was untouchable. Did the war paint on my pony tip the scales of victory?

The name and the new found confidence made Joe Lunchbucket and his *Dr. GO* a force to be reckoned with at the drag strip and on the street. Once the legend was loosed it seemed that there was no shortage of challengers. To be sure I accepted the challenges as they presented themselves; losing count after a while. Of course, I didn't win them all, but the won-loss percentage was high and in my favor.

I remember one particular night the word was out that the races were on at Ogden and Cicero Avenue; the raceway was actually on Ogden adjacent to Western Electric. The starting line was not far off Cicero Avenue and the race ended as we would start up the long bridge over the rail yards. Usually, lurking on the other side of the bridge were the Cicero police, salivating for the opportunity to catch two unsuspecting street racers coming over the bridge out of Chicago at what would be categorized as 'gross speed'! The Chicago Police on the starting side of the race were a) either non-existent (surely crushing crime elsewhere) or b) more accommodating and entrepreneurial. On this night the entrepreneurs showed up. There were war ponies and warriors on both sides of the street; a good guess would have been maybe a hundred cars and close to two hundred racers and spectators. The enterprising law enforcement officials smelled a big payday and told us to pass the collection plate. It was a hot summer night, we were ready to light them up, make some noise and, for at least half of us, win some money. We all anteed up to show our support for the law and managed just over a hundred bucks. The response was lackluster and the Chicago Blue said this is good for one race. Obviously, we all showed our disdain, but thought, maybe with one race to get the blood flowing we could get the contributions up and get a full evening in; after all, the police were good enough to block off Ogden at Cicero to accommodate the Friday Night Races! I know I was ready, so I pulled the Dr. into the starting position and awaited an opponent. No takers? The Dr. was completely painted and ready for another Sunday, so there we are again with tipping those scales. There was only one thing to do…stage a race. My friend John Tambolini from Berwyn with his GTO was ready to heed the call and paired up with me. A spectator stepped up to be the official starter and we were ready to get the evening races in to high gear. A good start and John and I were tearing up the make shift quarter mile heading for the bridge. A good race, a good start to the evening…or at least we thought. Prior to the race we had been warned that the Cicero Police were, in fact, waiting on the other side of the bridge. So, John and I did the only thing we could do to avoid certain arrest and ticketing. We slowed before the crest of the bridge and rolled backward back down to the race area. We had stepped up to get things started so when we returned to the race area we were ready to take our place as spectators. Unfortunately, there was not the expected outpouring of cash to continue the racing, as it turned out, that was the first and last competition of that evening; I closed up the headers and we quietly drove over the bridge and minded the speed limit, passed the waiting cavalry and returned to Tops for car and car hop watching.

Oswego was certainly one of my favorite drag strips and Sunday would not be the same without attending or racing the day away. From time trials to elimination racing, just being there was exhilarating and always great fun. The management of this drag strip had a flair for increasing the gate receipts with top name racers and exhibitions. All of these, however, paled in comparison to the fan favorite "Powder Puff Derby". If you missed this moment in drag racing you missed a real treat. It was a real drag race in all respects, except for the official start. Rather than the typical staging and countdown of lights to go, the ladies started about 10 yards in front of the cars and competed in a foot race to grab the keys off the passenger side front fender, run around the car, jump in start the car and blast down the strip. It was a Lemans start to a quarter mile; how novel.

Why the Lemans start? Is it because the ladies were not capable of a clean stage and start using the light tree? No way! There is no reason not to believe that any of these maidens could have brought the car to the staging area and successfully negotiated a clean start. After all, they were being entrusted with the successful driving of an automobile with obscene horsepower, racing modifications, manual transmissions, spinning tires and speeds in excess of 100 mph in just a very few seconds. Oh, I for one believe they were capable.

Hot summer days, running 30 feet, scrambling around and jumping into the car, starting and blasting down the drag strip was not an event for...let's be politically correct...someone that was vertically challenged. This started out as a foot race, not a 10 meter mosey to the car; these honeys had to be in good physical shape. What do you say we break this down? The goal is to get people to the drag strip, ergo increasing gate receipts. Drag racing (at least at the time) was a motor sport dominated by men.

Hot summer days, no shade, hot cars, hot babes in a foot race; we're not talking running around in a flame retardant racing suit…more like short shorts and blouses suitable for working on the all important summer tan. Remember a few chronicles back we covered the Top Graders and raging hormones? Still raging! Let me sum up: We have fair young maidens who are in great physical shape, sporting short shorts highlighting primo derrieres and blouses suitable for tanning offering maximum jiggle effect when running to grab the keys, run some more and jump into the awaiting race car. Do I need to add photos to the chronicle? I would submit to you that the race itself was anti-climatic at that point. Let's have a show of hands for those out there thinking the gate receipts may have gone up. There you have it, unanimous. Yes, folks this was no half baked promotional gimmick. It was fully baked!

Ok, so here we are on Sunday at Oswego Drag Raceway. *Dr. Go* is painted, tuned, headers open, slicks at 12 pounds of air, front tires at 60 pounds of air, the 3600 pound racing clutch adjusted, timing advanced, a new Hurst shifter and T-Bar dry and ready, at the staging area with the keys on the hood. All that is missing is the fair young maiden that is going to take the controls and blow the doors off the competition. In selecting just the right person to step up to this challenge the members of the *Dr. Go* Racing Team (that was pretty much me and Rich Rubeck) wanted someone with grit and determination; superior driving ability to handle the horsepower; someone that we could teach the fine art of power shifting; someone that was fleet of foot and highly coordinated with the keys and initial ignition (the start was everything); someone fearless…and most importantly she had to possess a primo derriere and a reckless abandon regarding maximum jiggle effect! We needed the total package, settling for anything less was never considered. Before we had the opportunity to set up tryouts and swim suit competition, our precursor to Danica Patrick offered her services. Ladies and gentlemen I give you...the woman, the myth, the legend...Gayle Vojta! As they say, the rest was history. Gayle was a solid drag strip queen and she won many a race driving the Dr. I am not sure if there were trophies or some other prize awarded, but regardless, Gayle secured her place in the lore and legend of drag racing and the 8 Corners.

There is no question in my mind that this chronicle has left out many a warrior, war pony and gear slamming race. Also without question the chronicle has not addressed or given justice to many other young 8 Corner damsels who qualified to race *Dr. Go* in all respects except grit and determination, superior driving ability, the ability to learn the fine art of power shifting, being fleet of foot and highly coordinated with keys and initial ignition and fearless. Gee, what have I left out?

A salute to all of the Mystic Warriors and their War Ponies of our youth! Some may remember the view of the tail lights of *Dr. Go*; to them I say; you ran a good race and better luck next time. For those whose tail lights I remember...I must have been behind you in line entering the drag strip...after that there were precious few.

CHAPTER **Seven**

It's Time to Party!

When growing up there was an apparent protocol estab-
lished to invite and attend a party. The customary ritual
was for the person having the party to send out invitations
and the invitees would then RSVP their intentions back to
the host or hostess. All of the usual information was provided; date, time, type of party. This protocol left little to
doubt. An invitee knew the logistics of the party and if a gift
was appropriate and what the dress code would be. These
heady details were negotiated and discussed at a higher
level…meaning our parents. Our task was to show up,
have a good time, enjoy the food and festivities and try not
to harm, in any way, the person on whose behalf the party
was being given or the environment of the host inside or
outside the home. This protocol worked well; as I am sure
it still does, when we were youngsters.

Fast forward the clock to the high school years and this
protocol was beginning to be replaced by a more informal process. Parties became a bit more impromptu. One
might ask their parents if it would be all right to have a few

of the gang over to listen to some music, indulge in conversation, maybe even dance a little to the latest romantic
melody. Menus at these gatherings may have been pizza or
just munchies and soft drinks. I clearly remember a few of
these soirées at the home of Charlie Smith. His basement
was well appointed, good stereo and sound proof enough
for his parents not to be too disturbed by the young lads
and lasses that were enjoying each others company. When
our band, the Sultans, was together the locale of these
festivities could be found at the home of Larry Spath, our
drummer. Even yours truly, Joe Lunchbucket, hosted a few,
although mine were mainly stag with the attraction being
to shoot pool for hours on end; all in all, very innocent.

At some time in those high school years the party
scene morphed to another level. It may have been, not
unlike man discovering fire or inventing the wheel, when
we first discovered adult beverages and stumbled onto the
methodology for accessing suitable quantities of it surrep-
titiously and under the cover of darkness! An older sister or
brother or an acquaintance that was of legal age always
seemed available to deliver the beverages of choice, usually for some fee or beverage quantity for themselves. They
were old enough to deliver the goods, ergo, they were
old enough to drive and drop us off at one of the local
"Groves" so that we might slip covertly into the shadows,
malted brew in hand, to sit quietly and consume our illicit
liquids. Did I say quietly? Well, that is how it began, but I
fear that by the time the last drop was consumed we were
more than a tad boisterous. Well, maybe we were bordering obnoxious. What a conversion. We went into the
Grove with great stealth. About an hour later we emerged
faster, smarter, stronger, tougher and better looking! We

were convinced that all the ladies wanted us and all the guys were mere wimps and we would squish them at the first sign of any disconcerting look. In retrospect, I fear we were rebuffed by most of the ladies and got our collective asses kicked more than once. Oh well, never in doubt, but seldom right, we partied on through those years.

Like anything else that is immoral, illegal or fattening we could not get enough of the continuous party. Weekends were just too far apart; what was needed was a place to convene during the week, maybe right after school and/or week-day evenings. It was just then that we were delivered unto John Bajor. This was perfect for a time. On any given day after school his house would be teeming with girls and guys in search of the endless party. It was not unusual to find thirty or more party animals at John's at any given time. We had a place out of the elements to relax, converse, imbibe, stash our adult beverages for future consumption and hit on the babe du jour. The cosmic tumblers had aligned and nirvana was at hand! John also hosted many of the guys after hours, after the dates had been returned to their upright positions and home safely. We would then rendezvous at John's for all night card games, tales of daring do and, of course, quaffing toward oblivion. How **did** we survive? Survive we did and we continued to hone our party detection skills.

When we became more mobile we moved on to Riverside, a target rich environment. In Riverside when one parks on those winding streets it was required to leave the parking lights on. Obviously, we had met and become friendly with many of the Riverside students at RBHS, so it was not unusual for us to catch the scuttlebutt about the parties on the docket for the weekend. Assuming we had a general bearing of where the party would be, then the parking lights functioned as a homing beacon to us. In due course we found that all we needed to do was wander the streets looking for the lights; we didn't even need to know about a party, and who cared about an invitation. All that was required was to walk in as if you were expected, blend in and find the nearest cache of adult beverage.

In comparison to our Brookfield parties the Riverside galas were extravaganzas! These parties were attended by most of the known civilized world...or so it seemed. On one occasion I remember finding a festive event in process (the parking lights); I parked my car and walked up to the front yard only to find the Riverside Police out in force. My initial reaction was "Damn, too late the cops have already shut it down!" Knowing how hard core partiers hate to give it up, I thought I would sort of stand in the shadows, wait for someone exiting the party and ask where the party would resume; as they always did. Much to my surprise, no one was leaving. Oh contraire, the masses kept entering. The Riverside Police were there to direct traffic to avoid any accidents and the host or hostess had her parents out in front collecting $2.00 for admission! Only in Riverside could this possibly happen. Once in, there were large boxes strategically placed throughout the backyard, lined with plastic, filled with ice and the mother lode...beer for all taste buds; no brand was unrepresented. There was no question that a good number of the RBHS student body would be feeling no pain as the evening progressed. Now these folks knew how to throw a party!

In the early days of the Sultans we applied our talents as the combo of choice to some of these parties. Those were the pre-salad days of the group when we would play for $2.00 to $5.00 per man and all the beer we could consume and still find our instruments. The exposure led to other gigs at local venues and we were on our way to become a band of some renown, but, the history of the Sultans is another story for another time.

Time marches on and even the Riverside parties were becoming old hat. We needed a fresh, bold party model. I am not sure how it was conceived or when, but just when needed that new model came along. Ladies and gentlemen I offer to you what back then became the next generation of full contact partying. Presenting the motel party! The working model was simple in design and execution. Amass a group of the young and carefree; those with a joie de vivre, take up a collection to cover costs, send someone of age out to rent a room or two (preferably adjoining), add adult beverages and there you have it...instant gala event! Without question a local Motel 6 or family owned dive would not fit the bill. Hey, we were a class group; we went for the suites at establishments out near O'Hare Airport. Little did they know that we were going to cram 40 or 50 people into their suite for an evening of non-stop revelry!

These parties were the stuff of legend and there was no room for Emily Post. We were there to party and take no prisoners. One could wander through the suite and find folks making wine snow cones in the bathroom. The bathtub filled with beer and ice. At one of these soirées Larry LaJeone, Dave Sanders and yours truly (Joe Lunchbucket), in search of the fame accorded to those highlighted in the Guinness Book of World Records, engaged in a three man Gin drinking relay. We drained a full fifth of some cheap Gin, straight from the bottle in less than 20 minutes. One should note that this was a couple of decades ahead of successful liver transplants, so we were boldly going where no man had gone before! There was no question that as we partied on into the evening the decibel level from our suite was registering close to 6.5 on the Richter scale. To add flair to our devil may care attitude, someone was ordering champagne from room service. Not a good idea. The third bottle came replete with the house security service cleverly disguised as the schmuck from room service; busted, party over. Never fear, we would live to party another day at another hotel and soon. This format was too good to discard just because of a minor infraction of some arbitrary rules made up by someone else!

A remembrance of one of these frenzied parties was recently brought to mind by Cathy Colgrass-Edwards. It was the usual fanfare at one of the hotels, nothing really unique or different. All were having a good time. Suddenly, someone noted that Gayle Vojta had disappeared. Interrogation of the guests sober enough to remember not only seeing Gayle, but who Gayle was, uncovered that she was last seen entering the bathroom. A quick check and sure enough the door was locked. It was noted that she was feeling rather down, her man was off in Viet Nam, so worry and a level of despondency may have been considered normal. Manley, being ever mindful and caring, was not going to take any chances that Gayle might be doing some unspeakable harm to herself, stepped back across the room and ran full speed ahead at the bathroom door. Let me set the stage here. Manley, although being quite nimble was, shall we say, of some bulk. What transpired in that split second was something right out of a cartoon. Blazing across that room full speed ahead at the locked door, Manley hit it in stride and went right through it. We're not talking taking it off the hinges, but smooth through the door…it remained locked and shut, just Manley's silhouette was taken out of the door. As it turned out Gayle was not doing herself in, she had just dozed off. The sound of fury of Manley coming through the door, however, was enough to give her cardiac failure, I'm sure. We were not invited back to that establishment again.

The model didn't change much as we partied on. We did start to bring our own records and record player to provide music suitable for dancing. Then there was the food and drink, and, of course, the burgeoning number of guests. The logistics of putting one of these forays into "impromptu" partying was beginning to resemble troop movements on, at least, a divisional scale. What pops into my mind today is "What can Brown do for you?"

This format remained in vogue until I departed for university life, at which time I was expatriated to southern Illinois and removed from the guest list. Of course, many of the revelers were getting married and setting up house, so the party scene adapted to the new quarters of the freshly married brethren. Yeah, that's right, they may have chosen their mates, but the party animals came along on weekends as part of the bargain. It's amazing that we all stayed friends through the endless intrusions on marital bliss. Jane and I can personally attest to the many lost weekends after we were married and moved into our first apartment. Living in Lyons, Illinois made our place a natural stop or starting place before beginning the real partying at the Purple Twig, the lounge of choice. The "Twig" replaced all of the previous venues. Most of us were still just shy of legal drinking age, but armed with outstanding faux IDs entry into the nightlife offered at the Twig was open to all. Besides, I am not sure the person checking IDs at the door could have read them had they been printed on a billboard. There were no more collections to get rooms, no more collections to pay for damages, no more need to secure adult beverages in advance. It had all the necessities: indoors, seating, adult beverages, live music and the only out of pocket cost were the drinks. So, getting a head start at someone's abode was nearly required, since most all of us lacked deep pockets.

I am sure this venue and others like it continued to satisfy the party needs for our group, but I was in queue for a different party; the US Army called. After which I returned to my studies and never really returned to the home front on any permanent basis.

I suspect that as night follows day many of the old gang fell by the wayside and abandoned the forever party lifestyle. However, fast forwarding about fifteen years and we all assembled for one of the earliest reunions of the group. Now with most of us pushing forty one would think a more sedate atmosphere would have been the modus operandi. To the contrary, we were as lively as ever. Music, laughter, food and drink were in abundance as we renewed acquaintances, enjoyed ourselves and killed a few more brain cells. Would we or could we expect any less? Of course not.

We continue these festive events to this day. My only regret is that we missed several by being incommunicado, if you will. It is always good to renew the friendships, tell tall tales and laugh until we cry. We're all mostly beyond the sixty age barrier and those that aren't, are probably carrying phony AARP IDs…it's just who we are. There is an old saying that growing old is mandatory, but growing up is optional. Dennis Hopper does TV commercials noting that our age group…Baby Boomers…is entering the retirement years kicking and screaming and as we enter those golden years we are looking for a plan to start something new; something that will keep us forever young. My gang has found it and we found it years ago and have hung on to it. Party on and stay young!

CHAPTER Eight

The Music Men

In a time long, long ago when rock and roll was still a fairly new genre of music, lyrics were understandable and there was a definitive melodic beat, the music, the times and the miracle of friendship and kindred spirits gave birth to a local combo. From the humble beginnings of four young lads, three with guitars and one willing to try pounding on a set of drums, grew a rock band that made its mark on the Chicago area music scene. Are we talking about the Fab Four from Liverpool? Well, in a word, no. While not destined to grow to a regional or national sensation, these young men carved out a niche and a following that is still fresh in the memories of those that knew, enjoyed and followed "The Sultans".

Noting that these were humble beginnings may be an understatement. I'm pretty sure our drummer had seen drums before, but had never actually played drums. Our rhythm guitar and yours truly were taking lessons, but still early on the learning curve. Thankfully, our lead guitar player, though mostly self taught, was advanced enough to give aid and comfort to us would be rockers. I was to be the bassist in this combo, yet I was bass-less. I did have a brand spanking used *Silvertone* guitar that had a fair bass range, but alas it was still a guitar. Something had to be done about this, if I was to look and sound official. Our lead guitar player, as I recall, had an old Fender Stratocaster; and I don't recall at all the make or model used early on by our rhythm guitarist...it may have been on loan from the music studio. And drums, well we didn't have some. How's that for humble? What we lacked in actual musical instruments and talent we made up for with sheer determination and positive mental attitude.

Having a four piece rock combo with a drummer sans drums presented a significant liability; knowing a chord from a note for the rest of us presented still another up hill struggle. We pressed on. Drums were purchased; a used three piece set. Not exactly the set-up one might see Ginger Baker peering over with several tom-toms, two bass drums, snare and a host of cymbals, but then again a starter set was apropos for a drummer who had not... drummed before. The rest of us would make do with what we had at the time.

Our first gig (we need to use the music jargon, if we are to get the true flavor of this story) was an afternoon backyard party played for friends. It's a good thing too. We were awful! There was no pay for this engagement, just some real life experience, and a few adult beverages (thankfully) and a dose of reality...let the humbling begin!

And begin it did; in earnest. We played several of these party gigs, improving as we went, but I fear our zest for becoming the next rock combo to be featured on American Bandstand was outweighed by our lack of preparation, practice and organization. Realizing that your average tissue and comb, kazoo band was a rung or two up the ladder from us we decided that what was needed was solid preparation. We each practiced on our own, but until we could focus on a list of tunes, practice those tunes and be able to perform them cold, we were going to end up taking a walk down Lonely Street with our next gig at the Heartbreak Hotel. Believe me, getting four wannabes to agree on a list of tunes was cause for gnashing of teeth. Not to mention, we needed to have enough for, at least two, but better yet, three sets. Obviously, landing more play dates with a one act show would prove to be problematic.

If one considers that back in the day the average length of a rock song was about 3 minutes and we wanted to be prepared for three 45 minute sets, then we needed a minimum of 45 different tunes. Then add the extra baggage that the tunes needed to be broken into some ballads, some up-tempo, some instrumental and some lyrical and this thing was beginning to take on a life of its own! Which, by the way, brings us to still another minor problem; the vocals. Here's the lowdown on that. The drummer singing the vocals was out; he had enough to do keeping an orderly beat and having his drumming sound like drumming and not just random pounding on old cans. Me, forget that idea. Oh, I could and did support with background vocals...I would have fit well as one of the PIPS...but as a lead singer I couldn't carry a tune in a bucket. Our lead guitar player, truth be told, made me sound like Frank Sinatra; so foiled again. That left our rhythm guitar player as the vocalist of choice. Actually, it was more like his turn in the barrel. He was indeed the best of the lot, but to be sure the Grammy for best male vocalist was safe for the foreseeable future.

OK, add that to the list of practice, preparation, and organization, talent at the vocal level. What we needed was someone that had pitch, tone, who could learn the vocals (having the words on a sheet of paper while you are singing is never acceptable) and showmanship. The hunt was on as the humbling continued.

We were diligent over an entire summer learning, practicing, honing our skills and putting together an acceptable show with a list of tunes equal to the task of three sets. There were still a handful of those songs on our list that were difficult for each one of us; luckily, for the most part, they were difficult individually and not collectively on any one song. For example, I remember one of our first real gigs…meaning the kind you actually get paid for…there was a song that had a fairly difficult bass run. Believing in the old adage that you have to fake it until you make it, I simply turned down the volume on my instrument to an inaudible level and acted as if the run was second nature. That's proof that people will hear what they expect to hear, even if it is not there.

As we pressed onward to fame and fortune, we were getting better. Our performances were actually beginning to sound like a real band, rather than just the garage band. We were also beginning to get better equipment. Our drummer bought a brand new set of Ludwig drums, our rhythm guitar player was now sporting a new Gibson Les Paul, our lead retired the Stratocaster for a new Fender JazzMaster and I picked up the bassists dream, a Fender Jazz Bass. Our sound was much better too. We were now pushing it through a Fender Showman and Bassman amps. But, alas, we were still short the talent we needed on the vocals.

If memory serves, we tried everything to find a suitable vocalist; asking everyone we knew, auditions, contemplation of exerting moral suasion on the singer of another band, groveling, consulting mystics and soothsayers, more groveling…you get the picture. This may have been the precursor to American Idol, and most of what we encountered was the talent found in the early stages of the selection process; tone deaf, off key and zero in the way of show-stopping personality. Can you spell humble?

The Sultans were near ready. We had purchased high dollar equipment. We had practiced relentlessly. Our sound was developing and the music was coherent and melodic. All we lacked was the upfront talent to keep the show going, the crowd engaged and belt out the tunes with some reasonable and respectable tone, pitch and tempo. Nearing the end of our rope, our summer Novena was answered and a crooner stepped up to the plate and offered his services. We gave him a list of our show tunes and an audition. I will admit that he would never be mistaken for the Velvet Fog (Mel Torme for those that are not devotees), but he could carry a tune, his pitch was acceptable, he knew the words without a teleprompter or queue cards and he was a sensational showman! He could keep the crowd engaged with his singing, his antics and his comedic sensibilities. Ladies and gentlemen, introducing Paul Slusarczyk, better known as Sluie, and *"Sluie and the Sultans"* was birthed! Here is the intro on the album cover, had there ever been one: Vocals Sluie, Lead Guitar with sensational riffs, Dave Sanders, Rhythm Guitar and pushing the beat, Larry LaJeone, Drums and setting the tempo, Larry Spath and Bass and pushing the bottom beat, yours truly Joe Lunchbucket. Look out in the world of rock! The new kids were on the scene and we meant to make a name for ourselves.

Without question more practice, an expanded playlist and the development of a "show" were high on the agenda now that the band was complete. We were still learning our trade and with an advertising budget of $0 dollars finding the killer gigs was problematic at best. We continued to play the no pay and low pay parties and nameless dances and, to our great fortune, word of mouth was beginning to take hold.

For a bunch of west suburban white kids we did a fair job on the Motown tunes, shone through on the early rock standards and added a new dimension with some adaptations and semi-original pieces. Two in particular stand out in my memory; the first being "Bongo Guitar" and the second was our rendition of the Ventures hit tune, "Last Night". Both of these were instrumentals. "Bongo Guitar" was more of a jazz piece than rock and it had a tendency to mesmerize the crowd. "Last Night" was a powerful driving beat that had a tendency to incite the crowd. Let me rephrase that. When we played that tune all the young lads in the crowd became bigger, faster, stronger and better looking than all the other young lads at the soirée… in other words, this tune usually started the light through heavyweight fights…all at once. Obviously, this tune was saved for our last set of the evening, so as not to cut the affair short.

Our arrangement and mix of the music, the growing quality of the overall sound and show and help from friends and (dare I say it) fans talking about us, and we were beginning to gain exposure and notoriety. However, something was missing that would put us over the top and get the solid gigs that led to fame and fortune. And then it happened. We received an offer from a friend and former performer to manage us. He had connections...he'd been there...he had experience and knowledge of music and the music scene, and most important to me, he became a mentor on perfecting my craft on the bass...his instrument of choice. Sluie and the Sultans were about to be propelled into the forefront of the local dances that were meaningful and beyond. Our humble beginnings and hard work came together with our own combination of Phil Specter and Dick Clark in the body of Cliff St. John. This addition to the entourage took us to a whole new level.

Cliff's input, expertise and connections put us in the best of the local dances; took us to new venues in the city and surrounding burbs and without question was getting us booked constantly and paid in real coin of the realm... no more playing for adult beverages. As we became better known and the gigs were coming with regularity, Cliff took on another facet in our musical world; he became a part of the performing combo as well as the manager. No, Joe Lunchbucket did not give up his spot as the bassist to become a roadie. Cliff purchased a Hammond organ, six foot Leslie speaker and a van to transport it. We were pre-Farfisa and synthesizers were not even on the RADAR yet, and this behemoth really added to the overall uniqueness of the Sultan sound. Humble was now in the rear view mirror and we rarely looked back!

Our playing days began in 1963 and continued on until sometime early in 1965. Through it all we played all of the major Brookfield dances, gigs large and small in Chicago and a long engagement at the semi-legendary, almost famous Red Bench in Downers Grove, Illinois. We met a lot of good folks along the way, curried some new friendships and brought a unique form of music and enjoyment to our loyal friends and fans. That said all good things come to an end for many reasons. We had our artistic differences, differing opinions about bookings and even thoughts about cutting a record, but ultimately it wound down because life goes on and other challenges and opportunities presented themselves. Now, some forty plus years later, the memories and sounds still linger in the recesses of my mind. The laughter and tears shared with my cohorts in music will always have a spot in my heart. These were good lads, good friends and a time in our lives to be cherished.

To Larry, Dave, Larry, Sluie and Cliff all I can say is BRAVO, BRAVO and BRAVO! Thanks for being part of, sharing and making this memory...the music of my... our...lives. How about a standing ovation for the **MUSIC MEN**!

CHAPTER Nine

Where Have They all Gone?

Bob Dylan had a hit song titled *"The Times They Are A-Changin'"*, and by the mid 1960's this was apparent to all of us at the 8 Corners.

By 1965, most of the group had graduated high school and was off to other adventures; work, college or married life. Regardless, of what direction lives were taking the carefree and raucous days began to wane. I was class of 1966, and found myself somewhat lost. The days of Sluie and the Sultans were over, old friends with new demands were no longer available, and instantly it seemed I had achieved Lone Ranger status. There were still the weekend escapades, but the old haunts of Steve & Grace and Manley's were bordering ghost town during the week, and somehow still being in high school became a significant liability. Feeling like a pair of brown loafers in a room full of tuxedos would cover the aura that was enveloping me. In retrospect and many years later, I feel that this time in my life propelled me toward some errant decisions that initially cost me dearly, but over the long haul paid dividends in discipline and character. Those errant decisions are better left collecting dust.

The timetables have been forgotten, but surely as night follows day many of the boys of the 8 Corners embarked on a new and dangerous journey into manhood. The Army took most of the eligible that had not gone off to school, although a few did opt for one of the other services. The disappearing act continued as the war in Viet Nam escalated. Each of our brothers has their own memories of their experience and I dare not attempt to tell their stories. So, this recollection, while singular in detail, may speak toward a more common reflection of a clear memory from a distant time and place.

After graduating from R-B (on the extended plan for the gifted students) in 1967, it was off to college. I was anything but ready for this. When asked what I was taking up in college, the truth be told, it was time and space. I faired all right in the studies, but Phi Beta Kappa was not vetting me for membership. Somewhere in that first year I met the young lady that would share the journey I have been on ever since and she would become Jane Lunchbucket. I can truthfully say that was the one good thing to manifest itself during that first year at the university. A year of studies under my belt found me wanting a change of scenery. Jane and I were planning a wedding, so having real jobs sounded like the thing to do. We suspended the pursuit of higher education to join the nine to five crowd and earn our way. Problem was I was young, healthy and now available for a more distant and exotic employment. Finding gainful employment was problematic and without my college deferment I was just marking time until I could start marking time officially on the payroll of our Uncle Sam.

It was a frosty morning in March 1969 when my tour of duty began. The alarm went off before the roosters were even awake and of all things I was awakened to the Star Spangled Banner. Quite fitting for the journey I was about to begin, but on this morning it struck me just off center and the clock radio paid the ultimate price as it sailed effortlessly through the air until impact on a nearby wall. Humor had escaped me on this day. Hey, it was 3:30 AM and I was getting on a fast track to the danger zone; would you be humorous at that point?

In retrospect the time in basic and advanced training passed quickly. Eight weeks at Fort Polk, Louisiana, which may be enough to convince anyone that Southeast Asia would be a step up, was followed by eight more weeks of learning RADAR with the cannon cockers at Fort Sill, Oklahoma. Fort Sill in the summer is just a few degrees hotter than what I imagine Hell to be. Advanced training complete and having become an expert scope dope I was ready to apply my new found skill registering outgoing cannon fire and charting incoming return fire from those swell guys on the other side. For any of my comrades in arms that spent any time as a forward observer you know that the RADAR assigned to our firebases (LZ) was doing essentially the same task. Therefore, in the grand scheme of things, we may as well have been wearing targets on our jungle fatigues. The only remaining training segment left to complete was the official Republic of Viet Nam combat readiness. This highly intense three days was complete with movies, rifle range, assaults on mock villages and some really nasty brown bag lunches. The brown bags should have been the first clue that this was not really preparing us for what was to come. Training done, orders cut, two weeks leave granted and it was time to get on with it; September 1969, destination Bien Hoa and assignment to a field battery someplace in south Viet Nam.

It's a long flight from sunny California to that lush tropical paradise bordering the South China Sea, and the closer we got to the end destination the more subdued the plane-load of troopers became. Two-hundred and eighty FNGs touch down early morning at Bien Hoa airfield. Less than fifteen minutes later the jetliner is taxiing back to the runway's end to get safely airborne. Its departure is less calm than its arrival. Almost on queue our less than hospitable hosts began incessant mortar fire in an attempt to take out the jetliner and anything else in the same zip code, not really, the Vietnamese didn't really have zip codes...I made that up, but I'm confident that you get the visual on this activity. My first thought was... SHIT, I'm in country less than 10 minutes and there are real bombs going off all around...this is going to be a very long year. As the panic and general mayhem began some authoritative figure announced on the base camp loud speaker that we should not attempt to assist in camp defense. I know my first thought was to run toward the sound of the explosions flailing a clean pair of OD Green socks in a best effort to intimidate those lobbing mortar shells at us. Yeah boy, they would have known there was a reckoning coming now...Joe Lunchbucket had arrived! As luck would have it, I quickly came to my senses and did my best impression of a gold medal sprinter to the nearest bunker to watch the fray that developed. When the Huey gunships appeared and defoliated the nearby jungle with their mini-guns, the ruckus stopped as quickly as it began. OK, we could breath easy our first 30 minutes were over and we only had another 8,759.5 hours left to serve... piece of cake.

We were quickly processed in as official FNGs and given temporary housing assignments at the Long Bihn Base Camp. We were told to change to jungle fatigues and report for duty assignments. Collectively we were thinking that we would now find out where we would be stationed. Well, not yet. Our duty assignments more closely resembled the activities of a chain gang. As for me, I managed the cushy duty of filling sand bags for bunker and perimeter defense. Sand bags need to be filled with...sand. Sand was outside the wire. So off we went leaving the friendly confines of the base camp to fill a couple of bazillion sand bags. Where were those OD Green socks to flail, just in case I had to go mano y mano with Charlie?

There we were about twenty green recruits armed only with entrenching tools and empty sandbags protected by one sergeant with one rifle. The thought occurred to me that he may be like Barney Fife and have but one bullet! What a day this was turning out to be.

Under the watchful eye of our armed combatant we filled sandbags the rest of the day. There were the occasional small explosion and the distinctive sounds of small arms fire during that lazy hazy day putting South Viet Nam in a bag. When these skirmishes broke out the air would fill with gunships and several repeated passes and blasts by the gunners and the excitement would dissipate. All the while our lone gunman was relaxed and seemed to enjoy watching our labors in the hot sun.

Task complete it was back to the safety of the base camp hopefully to relax and maybe even get something to eat. Well, I was wrong. The Army works in mysterious ways, so the next agenda item was a formation in the sun to get our orders for duty assignments in the field. It seemed as if we stood in this formation for hours. I do know that the sun gave way to a cloudy sky that rapidly turned into a rain like I had never seen before. I imagine Noah would be familiar with this sort of deluge. There we were like drowned rats as each in the formation was informed of where he was going and when he would leave. Orders given, we were released to get some chow and relax until we left for the field.

Many of the soldiers I had trained with were on the same flight and detail that I had been since leaving California, so we gathered up and went off to the mess hall first then the EM Club to drink heavily. Somehow sucking down several cold adult beverages seemed appropriate after the ordeal we had been through. Bordering at this point on sleep deprivation and physical fatigue it didn't take long to achieve a cheerful level of numbness. I did, however, have the presence of mind to write the day's experience in my diary and have several of my fellow sojourners sign off on the page to attest to the events. It was close to midnight when we finally left the EM Club feeling absolutely marvelous. Time for some desperately needed sleep. I was to leave at 4:00 AM on a flight to Pleiku, so I could get a full three and one half hours of peaceful slumber. Did I mention that the Army doesn't pay much attention to clocks? Some ogre came along and jostled me out of my soon to be REM sleep and informed me of a change in plans. I was leaving now. Now I realize that I was under the influence of some alcohol, but I was pretty certain that I had not slept for the full three and one half hours. A quick look at the old Timex and sure enough I was right. OK, so we have to perform on a little less sleep…fifteen minutes. Pack up, don the jungle fatigues and off to the flight line at 1:30AM. I'm ready, let's go! And go we did at precisely 4:00 AM. The upside to all of this was that in just a few hours I would have only 8,736 hours left in the unfolding nightmare.

We arrived at the airstrip in Pleiku around 8:00 AM. Nothing much to speak of, a hard pack runway and a few small wooden buildings out in what seemed like the middle of no where. Now what?

The gruff sergeant yelled out, "take a load off troops, we will wait here for the trucks, but first they have to sweep the road for mines between here and Camp Enari".

So we pulled up some floor and sat down to smoke an endless chain of cigarettes and wait. I for one prayed that they did a thorough job on the mine sweep. We were now in the central highlands of South Viet Nam. Not a very hospitable environment. One thing that impressed me was the smell. It was horrible. One assumes a new level of appreciation for the sanitation infrastructure enjoyed back home. Then again it could have been the savory aroma of the dog stew being cooked by the villagers just outside of the clapboard building we were occupying. By mid morning the road had been swept and we were on our way to Camp Enari, headquarters of the 4th Infantry Division near Pleiku. To add a little perspective, this area is known as the Ia Drang Valley; the same place immortalized in the Mel Gibson movie "We Were Soldiers", although that combat took place some 4 years before I was assigned. I suspect it hadn't changed much.

Once at Camp Enari we were outfitted for our tour. Meaning I was finally given a weapon...no further sock flailing would be necessary. Of course, the weapon was near useless until we could get to a rifle range and zero the sights for our eye. That would be next. A trip to the rifle range which was, of course, outside the perimeter of Camp Enari; we were now at least armed.

We formed up and the sergeant in command pointed and called out, "you and you take the point!" Struck by terror, I realized he was talking to me and the schmuck standing next to me. OK, let's recap. I'm just over 24 hours in country and already I'm John Wayne. Only 8,732 hours to go, I can do it!

On point, a dozen yards ahead of the rest of the platoon, M-16 at the hip locked and loaded and on full automatic, with vigilant eyes surveying the terrain just ahead for even the slightest of movement; movement that would unleash the sleep deprived fury of Joe Lunchbucket. (Wow, sounds like something out of William Faulkner). We arrived at the rifle range several hundred yards out and quickly got about the task of zeroing our weapons. When we were about ready to begin the final phase at the range, a quick kill exercise, the jungle came alive and we were visited by several families of Montagnard's. I suspect they were getting out of harms way knowing all too well what we were about to do next. After all, this was their jungle; their home and we were about to wander through part of it firing at will at pop-up targets that simulate actual bad guys. As we began the trek through the quick kill range our sergeant instructed us to shoot at all targets as they popped up and that if anyone else stood up shoot them too; there was no reason for any friendly to be out there. As long as I was on point I figured, what the hell go first. I did, scored well in the exercise and then blended into the platoon for safety. On our return, I thought it only fair to let someone else have a turn at being on point...why should

I have all the fun?

Rifle range complete and weapons ready it is time to head back to the base camp. Standard practice was to spread out the main formation in about five yard intervals two abreast and separated by about ten feet. Feeling safely tucked away in the middle this time with the sergeant just behind and to my left he suddenly halted the formation. He told us to freeze and not move. What's your first thought, ambush, land mines or some other danger just ahead? Danger just ahead it was. As the platoon frozen in our steps waited, the danger passed by just one trooper ahead of me in the line…cobra, but the sergeant assured us it was a young one, not more than six to eight feet in length. Being put on point or in the middle of the platoon I, Joe Lunchbucket, seemed to be attracting all that life could bring on his big adventure to southeast Asia. We made it back to Camp Enari bullet hole and bite free and were given time off to spruce up and get ready for a variety show starring George Jessel that afternoon. A welcome break from what was now the better part of two full days, still without sleep. The show was fun, Jessel performed his stand up comic routine, there was music, and it reminded all of us that we were far from home and in a very strange place for the year to come and pretty much detached from any reality we had ever known.

The entertainment ended, we got some fairly good chow and we were off to bed down for the night. Tomorrow we would link up with our assigned units. Finally, we were in a barracks, we had a cot and were desperately longing for a full night's sleep without interruption. I lie down on the cot, exhausted and determined to forget about the last thirty-six hours since I stepped off that plane. My eyes closed and drifting effortlessly off to a better place when that sound that I had come to know so well at Fort Sill broke the silence that we were enjoying. It was the high pitched whistling sound of a heavy artillery shell. OK we're upright again, jungle boots on and running for the nearest bunker and looking like typical FNGs…jungle boots and Army issue OD green boxer shorts; eat your heart out GQ! I'm almost to the bunker when I am grabbed by a young specialist laughing his ass off at the spectacle we were providing all those veteran troopers. He stopped me and yelled out…"Back to your bunks, it's outgoing fire!" A lullaby of 105 mm howitzers is not a good prescription for peaceful sleep. Back in the bunk I check the Timex, it's around midnight; just under 8,720 hours left, no problem, I'm tough, I'm gung ho, just let me get a little sleep and I'll face tomorrow head on.

There were three of us that went to Pleiku and assigned to the 6th of the 29th Artillery. I was assigned to the Headquarters Battery with the RADAR unit the others to B and C Batteries respectively, they were cannon cockers. We were wondering where in Camp Enari our unit was when the duty officer told us to pack up, weapon, ammo and duffle and be ready to travel in thirty minutes. The 6th/29th was in An Khe and we were on the road again. We board the back of the lone deuce and a half truck en route to An Khe and as we board the duty officer tells us, "lock and load boys, you're the defense on this near 80 mile ride through treacherous territory". There we were three FNGs, in the back of a lone truck sitting on top of mail and supplies weapons at the ready, off as for a Sunday drive in the country. Now, before and since I have taken the customary Sunday drive, but never have I had an M-16 in hand and two bandoliers, sixteen clips, strapped across my chest just in case of bad traffic. The drive from Pleiku to An Khe offered your usual scenery of destroyed trucks, downed helicopters and other signs of destruction from USDA explosives; same as the morning commute in any town in America. We collectively breathed easier once inside the base camp in An Khe and felt somewhat more secure now that we were with our units.

Upon meeting my new commanding officer, a second lieutenant, I snapped off my best stateside salute and the proper military reporting for duty greeting. This was met with a, "that was nice, but don't ever do that again and never call me sir". He told me I could call him Louie (short for lieutenant), by his first name Paul or even **hey you**, but never sir or Lieutenant; seems he didn't want to be a target. A RADAR unit is pretty close knit since it is a small squad consisting of the Lieutenant, a couple of repair technicians and three scope dopes (me included), so it is informal to say the least. We did not have a permanent billet in the base camp as our normal duty station would be out at a firebase, so we had taken up residence in the mail room of the 6th/29th Arty, and we were trying to stay low and avoid any chain gang type duty that might come along until we moved out to the field. Work wasn't totally avoidable. I was nabbed for KP in the general's mess and a day building sidewalks out of old ammo boxes. It helped to pass the time until the Louie could get us an assignment at one of the outlying LZs. After just a few days orders came in for us to deploy to LZ Patricia. The two repair technicians went out to dig what would become our home for the foreseeable future. Another technician and I were given the task of appropriating roofing material for our bunker. The roofing material consisted of sheets of PSP, which is interlocking sheets of perforated steel that was used along with sand-bags to build a protective space for the helicopters when on the ground. Each sheet is about ten to twelve feet long and weighs maybe a couple of hundred pounds. I know I wouldn't want to make a career out of loading these sheets into a truck like we did that day. I might note the sheets we secured were not extra or scrap. Somebody's Huey would be missing their protective cocoon when we were finished. We just had to hide the evidence until we were out of the base camp.

The next morning we were packing up to leave and it was raining really hard, so the Louie decided that we would take only what we had in the truck and leave the gas trailer behind…he didn't want to get it stuck in the mud when we went off the main road to the LZ. Good choice, wet muddy roads and a trailer with 450 gallons of gasoline was a recipe for disaster. We would come back for the gas, the generator and the RADAR as soon as we finished building the bunker and the road had a chance to dry out. We left the top off of the deuce and a half and the Louie and I took up our positions atop the newly appropriated roofing ma-terials and assorted supplies and left for LZ Patricia, some sixteen miles away out in the jungle. It was an uneventful journey until we came to a small village where we turned off the main highway on to a dirt road leading to the LZ. There we had to hold up until the infantry protection could sweep the road of land mines between their post and the village. Mines, why does it always have to be mines?

The LZ was a fair distance from the main road, so our wait was lengthy. In retrospect, it was less than a stellar idea for four US soldiers to be parked off the main road adjacent to a small Vietnamese village…does the term sitting duck hold any meaning here? Obviously, we became the focal point for village curiosity and it did not take long for some of the villagers and children to meander over our way. The sight of our M-16s stopped most in their tracks as they came closer. However, a few of the overly zealous thought boarding our truck would be something akin to a friendly gesture. They were wrong. As one head popped up over the truck siding he got an up close and personal look at the business end of my M-16. Apparently that close inspection of the muzzle was all he needed to see. Satisfied that I had cleaned it well and it was loaded he made an excellent decision and dismounted from the side of the truck and returned fairly rapidly to his village. We could only hope that this was a friendly village, although that could not be guaranteed, and since it was the four of us against the world we decided at that point a strong and intimidating military posture was the best approach.

About an hour after our arrival the infantry squad that was sweeping the road for mines arrived. The first thing that sort of jumped out at us was that they didn't have any mine sweeping equipment. Louie, somewhat perplexed, asked, "Just how they swept the road". The response was not exactly inspiring.

The squad leader replied with, "We walked along abreast and kept a visual for trigger devices".

Swell, these guys didn't step on anything that blew them into the stratosphere so it must be safe. What's up with that? Were we supposed to know the road was not clear if we heard the explosion and saw bodies flying through the air? Then the next squad would only have to sweep from the site of the last carnage? Second, the bad guys were adept at setting mines that would not go off even if a soldier walked right over it. Their whole idea was to set it for the pressure exerted by a truck in hopes that they could score more devastation than just one trooper. Oh well, this was as good as it was going to get, so we helped the squad aboard and started the drive back to their post just about 100 meters outside the perimeter of the LZ. Butts in the puckered position the drive to their post was uneventful. We dropped them off and began the final 100 meter drive to the LZ. About half way to the LZ from the listening post the LZ came into view and the Louie looked at me and said, "That's going to be home for the foreseeable future". As I turned to look, KABOOM! Go figure, the land mine was placed between the last listening post and the LZ... clever. Nobody swept the road the in other direction. The last thing I remember after the loud noise was one of the other members of our unit shielding me and telling me, "Here it comes again". This was followed by being pelted by what felt like thousands of needles. It was later that I found out that this was caused by the rotor blades of the Chinook that was coming in to medivac us out of the area. Fade to black.

Two days later I started to wake up, but was somewhat delirious, confused and not sure I wanted to open my eyes. As I opened one eye I noticed a young lady at a station next to the very comfy bed I was laying in. Having grown accustomed to an Army cot that was as comfortable as sleeping on gravel, my first thought was, "Wow, we dug one hell of a bunker"! I quickly jettisoned this thought pattern and asked the obvious question, "Where am I"?

The young lady responded with, "You are in the 67th Evac Hospital in Qui Nhon".

This response resonated because of the term EVAC; with gazelle like speed I quickly determined that this meant a ticket back to the world. That rationalized the next thought was, am I going home with all my pieces parts, and what happened? I decided to postpone any gruesome medical report and focused on what happened. I asked the ever profound question of this nice young lady, "What happened"? Her response was that she really didn't know as she was just the nurse caring for us in this wing of the hospital, but that I may want to ask my neighbor. Looking over to the next bed I found Louie. He seemed alert, so I thought I would take "What happened?" out for another spin.

Louie filled me in on all the details. We had run over a land mine 50 meters away from the LZ. It was powerful enough to twist the deuce and a half in two and blow all of the axels off. He departed the truck in one direction making a landing about 50 feet away, coming down hard in the sitting position, broken back. He related how I flew the other direction landing pretty much face first about 50 feet in the other direction. Unfortunately, the PSP (those long interlocking sheets of steel that we were carrying to use for our bunker roof) took the same route that I did and two of those sheets landed with me just a half second behind. Nothing like getting hit with some 400 pounds of steel to ruin your day, that's what I always say. The two unit members in the cab of the truck were not hurt and they had a bird's eye view of the whole ordeal. I missed it all because the mine went off directly under the wheel I was riding over. The concussion of the blast pretty much knocked me out of it. Thinking back to that day it was fortuitous that we did not bring the gas trailer along. Adding 450 gallons of gasoline into this explosive mix would have changed our outcome considerably.

OK, we had the answer to the "what happened" question; time to focus on the pieces parts question. I could see my arms and it seemed reasonable to assume that my head was attached, since I was engaging in conversation. I could not, however, feel my legs. A quick peek under the sheets and sure enough, still attached, that's a good thing. Obviously, the PSP had come down flat or I would be much shorter today. Flat was bad enough. Here's the graphic. Hard ground, Joe Lunchbucket, two sheets of steel all arriving at the same place in rapid succession with me sandwiched in between the ground and the steel. I was hit in the lower back with this steel and the result was a broken back and pelvic, broken nose and various other cuts and contusions. FUBAR is the term that comes to mind. This confluence of events was the reason for not being able to feel my legs. Information overload coupled with the nice young lady giving me another injection of morphine for the pain and I drifted back into my special place.

I was in and out for the next few days, mostly out, due to the drugs I am sure. At one point I did wake up to find my bed surrounded by doctors and cameras and a tall man who was shaking my hand while the cameras clicked away. I focused in on his shirt collar and noted there were four stars. He was about to pin a medal (Purple Heart) and I looked at him and recommended the sheet might be the best place, since I was not wearing a shirt; he agreed. The cameras were to record this for Stars and Stripes, but I got a nice Polaroid out of the deal…me and the general.

The doctors at the 67th decided I was movable after a few days and were sending me to the Cam Ranh Bay Army hospital for transport home. That was the good news. The bad news from their perspective and medical work up was that I could probably cancel my ballroom lessons at Arthur Murray; they were pretty sure that walking was an historical pursuit for me. How comforting. I had just told Jane Lunchbucket that I thought roller skates would be a good gift for me for Christmas too.

A stop over in Cam Ranh for a few days then on to Tokyo and the Army's 249th General Hospital for more tests and observations. I was departing Viet Nam having given it my all. Some get to all sooner than others. It appears I got to 'all' 8,256 hours sooner than the Army had anticipated.

We flew into Yakota Air Base and then had to be transported to the 249th by helicopter. This gave me a nice view of the city below from my stretcher/basket that was tied down between the airframe and the landing struts of the Huey. A little more open air than I like, but certainly a memorable flight.

My stay in Tokyo was mostly uneventful with the exception of Captain Smith. Captain Smith was a Cobra pilot who was shot down and pretty banged up; mostly head injuries. He was out of it most of the time and when he was awake he was only lucid about 20% of the time. One day he added some excitement when he decided he was going to have a cigarette (it was OK to smoke in the ward). Old Captain Smith lit his cigarette and then lit his bed on fire; after which, he promptly returned to his state of unconsciousness. This was not good. I grabbed my nurse call button and rang away as if we were under attack. The nurse came running to my bed, oblivious of the smoldering linen on Captain Smith's bed and scolded me for being so impatient, then asked what the problem was. I responded with, "Oh nothing for me, thank you, but you may want to get a fire extinguisher for Captain Smith and localize the inferno before it gets really nasty". She turned, looked, gasped and ran for the extinguisher. Once the fire was quelled she promptly took Captain Smith's cigarettes and lighter and posted signs on all four posts of his bed informing all who passed by to refrain from giving Captain Smith anything flammable.

In my way of thinking Captain Smith was now in my debt. I did, after all, save him from crashing and burning a second time, while he was on terra firma, and I had just the pay back in mind. Since the untimely explosion that put me into this predicament my diet, for reasons unknown to me had been chicken broth, tea and strawberry milk shakes. This was not by choosing, this was deemed appropriate by the Army medical staff. And, this wasn't for just some meals, it was every meal; breakfast, lunch and dinner. This was really getting to be unacceptable and called for covert action. Next meal due to be served was breakfast and I fashioned my plan then laid in wait to execute it the next morning. Early morning and the orderlies were passing out the standard faire for breakfast. You guessed it; I once again received my ration of chicken broth, tea and a strawberry milk shake. Captain Smith scored big with the full monty of eggs, bacon, hashed browns, toast, coffee and juice…a freakin feast and he was off in his usual twilight zone! It was time to strike and with all the poise and stealth I could muster I scooted over as far as I could in my bed. It was just far enough so I could snatch Captain Smith's fragrant and inviting breakfast off of his tray table; mission accomplished. But wait, I couldn't get caught with his breakfast on my tray table, that would surely mean a firing squad or worse. Hey, it was solid food for the first time in over a week and it was in my possession, there was no time to consider enjoying this and letting it envelop my shriveling taste buds, this had to be a lightening strike get in and get out. I must have looked like a hamster, stuffing that food in as fast as possible. This was a whole new era of fast foods. OK, food gone, I had to return the tray back to its original tray table. Deftly I managed to return the tray without detection. A few minutes latter Captain Smith woke up and he was in one of his lucid moments. This could spell trouble and called for quick thinking. I grabbed my strawberry milk shake and looked at the captain with the best forlorn look I could muster and said, "I sure wish they would get me off this liquid diet and feed me real food like they do you. How was your breakfast this morning captain?"

He looked at his empty tray and queried, "What happened to my breakfast?"

To which I replied, "You woke up a few minutes ago, wolfed it down then drifted back off to sleep, don't you remember?"

"Oh yeah, it was pretty tasty", he replied; then off to another spin around his twilight zone.

Operation Breakfast Stealth was a complete success, unfortunately it was a one time operation and I was back to the liquid diet. To this day, some 40 plus years later, I still cannot face a strawberry milk shake. It was a great weight loss program I have to admit. I went to Viet Nam weighing in at 175 pounds, when I returned home I tipped the scales at lean, mean 112 pounds. The weight reduction plan took all of three weeks. Don't tell me you can't lose those few extra pounds ladies. All you have to do is have three squares of chicken broth, tea and strawberry milk shakes for several weeks.

After a week in Tokyo it was back to Yakota Air Base and evacuation home. Lying in my bunk at the air base I saw one of the cannon cockers that went to the 6th/29th Arty with me. His leg was all shot up and he too had a ticket home. It was his battery that we were headed for to set up our RADAR when we were wasted, so I was more than mildly interested in what happened. Several nights after our encounter the LZ was without full infantry protection and they were overrun by Viet Cong. Seventy-five percent killed and the rest wounded. Glad I missed that part of the platinum tour of the countryside. I inquired about the other trooper that was assigned with us and he confirmed that his battery was in a fire fight and he paid the ultimate price. Three FNGs assigned and in a matter of weeks, all departing Viet Nam. What a waste.

The next day I was put on a transport home; a fuel stop in Alaska, an overnight at Scott Air Force Base then on to the hospital closest to home; Great Lakes Naval Hospital. At each hospital stop the medical staff had confirmed walking would not be an option. After a while you sort of come to grips with that diagnosis, but still fight not to believe this could happen. When I arrived at Great Lakes the attending physician ordered more x-rays of my back to determine treatment going forward so I would at least be able to sit up. The x-ray technician put me on a gurney and took me to the lab. During the x-ray session he tried to roll me over on my side for a lateral view and the pain was excruciating. He asked where the pain was originating and I indicated that it was around my hips. Apparently, this gave him an idea and he took an x-ray of my hip region. This technician had to be my Guardian Angel. It was he that first discovered that along with my broken back I suffered from a hairline fracture of my right pelvic bone. This was what was preventing me from moving my legs and having very little if any feeling. There was new hope thanks to this attentive technician!

My joie de vivre was returning with this latest revelation. The doctors consulted, poked, prodded and decided that a full body cast would be an ideal solution to immobilize the compression fractures of the vertebrae that I suffered. There was another patient in the ward that was encased in one of these plaster suits and given his demeanor I thought that I would ask for an alternative. The recommendation was a three point pressure brace. Proof that you never want to blindly accept what is behind door number one. This was not a comfortable resolution, but light years ahead of the body cast. Sold! The doctors also thought that I would be able to maneuver on crutches once the back brace was fitted. It was imperative to go slow and easy on the hairline fracture of the pelvic so that it might heal without further problems. This sounded great to me.

So, here I was bed bound in the Great Lakes Naval Hospital, October 1969. My brace and crutches were not due in for about a week and this was not a very pleasant piece of news. My birthday was coming up fast and the thought of celebrating my twenty-first birthday in a hospital ward was, to say the least, not very uplifting. I knew Jane would visit me and bring some birthday cheer, but still, how festive could it be in a ward full of surly, broken warriors? On my birthday Jane did show up and she did bring some cheer. She not only brought herself, but some of the gang from the 8 Corners too, with a huge birthday cake and plenty of good wishes!

I can still see Manley toting in that huge cake. It was a sheet cake and if memory serves he baked it and decorated it himself at his restaurant. The rest of the entourage included Linda, Cathy and, perhaps, a few others...hell it has been over forty years and some of this is packed way deep in the memory banks. Regardless, they came and we celebrated and my twenty-first birthday was a memorable one. The whole ward enjoyed the cake and the company nearly as much as I did. Looking back this was another one of those magical moments that bound us all together for a lifetime.

The day finally did come when the brace and crutches were provided. It took about a week to garner enough balance and leg strength to not only stand up, but to become ambulatory. I worked diligently at building strength and stamina and finally the doctors thought it would be all right to turn me loose on a weekend pass. It was good to be home to visit with the family, but when Saturday night rolled around we had to find a way to meet up with the gang. Back in those days the meet up place was Stein's in Lyons, so that was our first stop and we were able to surround ourselves with good friends, good cheer and plenty of laughs.

By the end of the weekend and upon my return to the Naval Hospital I was ready to lose the crutches. At rounds on Monday morning the attending asked how it went over the weekend. I told him, "Doc, lets trade in these crutches for some roller skates, I'm ready!" Well, maybe down from roller skates to maybe a cane, but I was walking on my own. Not bad for a guy who several weeks before was given the prognosis of watching the world go by from the sidelines. I did progress fairly rapidly and thought the convalescing would stretch until after the first of the year and then probably a discharge from duty. That was not in the cards. Instead of recuperating until January and then getting out, the Army decided that I was to return to duty, limited as it would be for some time, and I received orders to report to Fort Bliss, Texas by December 14, 1969... Merry Christmas. As it turns out there was a method to the madness. William Beaumont General Hospital was the best orthopedic facility the Army had at the time and it was time for serious physical therapy and follow up medical observation and treatment; so there was a positive to these orders. The sad part was once again leaving our family and friends behind to go off on still another adventure.

Sort of like Bilbo Baggins, my story took me "to there and back again" and it ended with recuperation and a future filled with promise. I salute all the other young men from the 8 Corners who shared this common experience. Most of us returned, some did not; and still others returned, but were never again the same personality that they were before leaving. Viet Nam changed us, it changed everything. It also brought a close to that decade of the 1960's and ushered in a new era for the 8 Corners Gang. Although we may not have realized it then, what we had gone through in the years leading to graduation and beyond had cemented relationships that, for the most part, have endured and will continue to endure.

Thank you for staying with me on this chronicle. It has not been the typical reminiscent story filled with humor and tales of daring do, but it is part and parcel of who we were and what happened to each of us and collectively.

Perhaps, it will provoke others to take a critical look at their service and help put things in perspective some four decades later. The Joe Lunchbucket story is just one, but shares a common thread with many.

CHAPTER Ten

The Hooligan Booth

In college I participated in an Inter-Greek festival. It was one of those activities designed to help the fraternities, sororities and other campus student groups raise money to advance their organization's objectives. In reality it was a way to raise money to continue partying until we graduated and had to become responsible, productive citizens.

It was in the spring that we collectively agreed that a carnival would be a tremendous way to have fun and redistribute money from the general student population to the treasuries of the various organized student groups. It would be a typical carnival complete with unstable rides, culinary delights that would make a goat puke and a host of games of chance. The organizations involved focused on the real money makers; food and games of chance.

After a long winter and prior to finals week, a carnival would be a wonderful diversion from education. Money that had gone unspent through the winter months was longing to be set free on an opportunity to eat something other than cafeteria vittles and a chance to win a cuddly, valueless animal for the girlfriend *du jour*.

Our task, call it a marketing program if you will, was to design a game that brought the players to brink of actually winning. Human psyche finds it difficult, if not impossible, to walk away from an opportunity that offers a challenge and the possibility of success for just one more quarter (not unlike the lotteries run by the several states). Besides, all of the 'would be' *bon vivants* had their own agendas and winning the cuddly was the key that may unlock the rite of spring.

Research indicated that our game had to be:

- Easy to understand;
- Presumably inexpensive to play;
- Immediately habit forming; and,
- Give the illusion of being beatable.

Enter the Hooligan Booth!

For one quarter a player could choose a lucky number between one and six and roll a handful of dice in an attempt to win a choice of prizes. The rules were simple. One roll of six dice. Count the number of dice that came to a stop with your chosen number and if your number showed up at least three times you won a prize...a bottle opener. If your number came up four times, you were free to select from a variety of beer mugs one mug emblazoned with your favorite brand of beer. As long as that brand was Budweiser, Busch, Miller or Pabst Blue Ribbon (more market research). A count of five garnered a small throw rug cartooned with the philosophy of the day...'Keep On Truckin'. Six like numbers in one throw was like achieving Nirvana. Your choice of the cuddly.

Crowd control and disgruntled players had to be taken into account. We allowed no more that eighteen players at a time. Three players could plunk their quarters down on each and every number. The quarters were then quickly and adeptly swept away and replaced with washers tied to a string. One contestant would then roll the dice for the entire wagering mass. The dice would come to a stop and the winners would be determined; if any. Usually someone would win a bottle opener. And surely, if three like numbers could come up, then the next roll would produce four, five or six like numbers. Another quarter please.

The hook had been set. The Hooligan Booth was easy to understand. It was "inexpensive" to play. It was immediately habit forming. It was impossible to beat!

We had assured ourselves of the first rule of wagering. The house must win.

This was accomplished by spending an afternoon rolling the dice, counting the numbers and then setting the level to win at a point where we would give away a great number of bottle openers. The chance of winning any other prize was remote at best. The cuddly? Once in a blue moon! Further, we had guaranteed profitability by quickly removing the quarters and replacing them with washers. A change of heart by a loser would not interfere with our money incentive. Hell, he couldn't even take the washer; it was tied to a string and attached to the booth!

Had we been math majors, we would have eliminated the need to waste an afternoon counting dice. This could have been calculated through statistical analysis. Actually, we did do the statistical calculations too, but we wanted absolute proof that the numbers would not come back to haunt us once the game was in full swing. After all, we had to pay for the prizes given away. The prizes were pur-chased on a contingency basis, by the way. So we paid for only those given away and not those returned.

The profit motive should be obvious. Giving away a bottle opener kept players at the booth relentlessly trans-ferring quarters from their pockets to our coffers in the pursuit of the cuddly. After a time, behavior modification set in on our victims. Sort of, "Well, if I can't win a cuddly, then at least I'll win a beer mug." Do we need to review the statistical analysis?

Bottle openers had a cost of five cents each. If every-body won a bottle opener, our profit was 400%. However, with six dice only two numbers could possibly come up as winners. At our maximums this would mean six winners (three at each of the two winning numbers). An outlay of thirty cents for the Booth and an income of $4.50. That translates into 1500% profit! The Hooligan Booth was an enormous success. It may still rank in the top ten of all fraternal money makers.

This was living proof that my quest for a degree in Economics was not a wasted effort; the Business School at Southern Illinois University had in fact succeeded in turn-ing out another young capitalist!

Fast Forward - The variations of the Hooligan Booth are many, but the end game is always money oriented. The Hooligan Booth puts a name on the 'extraction point' where my money is extracted from your pocket. Of course, I am using 'my' and 'your' to define the players, not to call attention to **moi**. As we race forward nearly 40 years we can see that there were others that had learned this concept well, but unlike yours truly, these folks continued to apply the concept relentlessly and ruthlessly to the detriment of the unsuspecting unwashed masses (that would be most of us). Our headlines are filled with the present day culprits: Bernie, AIG, Wall Street, Congress (both sides of the aisle) just to name a few.

So the next time you take your family to a fair, carnival or amusement park where games of chance are beckoning you with the lure of winning that cuddly for your spouse *du jour* you have been forewarned. Joe Lunchbucket has given you a look behind the curtain. The game is <u>easy</u>, seemingly <u>inexpensive</u>, <u>habit forming</u> and <u>unbeatable</u>.

Step right up! Got a quarter? Let's play again!

CHAPTER Eleven

The Little Red Tool Box

This morning I went out into the drive to secure the Sunday morning newspaper. It was enormous. As I picked up the 40 pounds of fresh newsprint, I reflected upon days gone bye when we did not have access to all the information known to man on any given subject to digest with our Sunday morning coffee. But then I thought this is just another assault designed to complicate our lives. Indulge me for a few minutes as I recount an adventure that took place in January 1993. An adventure with my youngest son when I first reflected that there was a simpler time.

The sun shone clear on Saturday morning and the temperatures rose to a level suitable to engage in a few outdoor tasks. What a change. Just ten short days ago the rains came while the mercury dipped below the freezing mark. The results had been a wintered landscape of ice sculptures and trees glistening. The season's beauty also exacted its toll. Next to our driveway laid the remains of a mighty pine branch broken off by the freezing rains. Today's job would be to clean it up. The plan was easy.

Cut the downed branch into firewood, and stack the tiny limbs near the curbside for removal by the city haulers. What I lacked was the proper tool for the job. A bow saw would do it; sounds like a trip to Sears. I rounded up my son and off we went on our adventure. Nothing better on a Saturday morning than for a man and his son to share an excursion among the hardware isles at the local Sears, and throw in a few side trips along the way.

We found the bow saw displayed with other yard tools, and my little helper wondered why it was not to be found with the other saws. Different tools for different jobs, I replied. Bow saws were an outdoor job kind of tool, the kind that went along with rakes and hoes and hedge trimmers. Other saws were destined to be carpenters or plumbers apprentices.

"Well, dad, what is a hack saw; what does it look like?"

So off we went to another isle to find the saws that are cousins to the bow saw, so my little helper would know the difference. This is male training not found in the everyday parent manuals, and surely, overlooked by all mothers. While we were in the area, I decided to look at a new toolbox. I have had my eye on this red beauty for two Christmas seasons. It was on sale. As we mused over and fondled the drawers and cabinets of this altar of manhood, I concluded that it would have to wait.

"Your mom would ask me if I had lost what was left of my mind, if I spent the hundred plus dollars tagged on this gem", I said to my son.

We paid for the bow saw and left the temple Sears. As we backed out of our parking space, I remarked, I should have bought it; well, next time.

"That's what you said last time, Dad", came impishly from the other seat.

"I know, but next time."

We were off to our next stop. It was a beautiful day, and it seemed the right time to stop at the car wash and rinse away the months of road dirt accumulated through the stormy weather. This is really where the story begins. We were greeted by a young official looking lad toting a clipboard and order pad. His inquiry was to what kind of wash we were interested in on this fine day. Did we want the Bronze, Silver or Gold treatment? Each had an expanded array of offerings. I chose the Bronze.

"And, what fragrance would you like?"

I chose baby powder, but I must admit I was ready to ask if they had BARNYARD ANIMAL. What was going on?! When I first began driving I took the car to the local wash to get it clean. There were no choices. Simply pull up, get out, pay your $2 or $3 bucks and wait on the other end. Now it's a menu approach, complicated, and ranging in price from $7.95 to $15.95. Madison Avenue has hit the car wash! Next we will be greeted by Halston clad young ladies asking if we choose to share the fantasy and deodorize our car with Chanel #5. Inside will be Tuxedoed Chip and Dale young men escorting us on a tour through the racks of velcro ash trays, plastic cup holders, stereo add-ons and imported wine....please have a glass of Chardonnay while we Armor-All your interior. I just wanted a clean windshield and shinny bumpers.

This surreal experience caused me to ponder. This sort of activity has permeated the entire fabric of our society. Go back to yesteryear when going to McDonald's was for a hamburger. Your choices then were: with or without cheese, do you want fries, and, small or large Coke? Today, ordering at McDonald's requires a degree in Astrophysics. Consider that you must negotiate through a menu that includes: hamburgers, cheeseburgers, quarter pounders with and without cheese, double cheeseburgers, Big Macs, McChicken sandwich, imitation rib foodstuff, chicken McNuggets, salads, breakfasts, 47 different sizes of fries, 5 different sizes and 30 flavors of drinks, cones, sundaes, cookies, happy meals, sad meals, value meals, limited offers, toys, movies, real estate and commodity futures. Make your selection and you will be asked: is this for here or to go, do you want a lid on your drinks, how many nuggets, 6, 9, 15 or enough to feed a brigade of starved 10 year olds, will you need honey, mustard, or special sauce for the nuggets, ketchup for the fries, salt, napkins, straws and may we suggest a hot apple pie to compliment your cuisine today? My final exam in advanced Microeconomic Theory was easier than trying to get lunch!

I should have asked for Barnyard Animal fragrance. And, on my next trip through the fast food, when they inquire if the order is for here or to go, I think I shall reply as the modern day philosopher and comedian, Steven Wright, would reply: No, I'm going to eat this in another dimension. I'd tell you about it, but your head would explode. In either case, I doubt anyone would notice.

I should have bought the toolbox!

CHAPTER Twelve

Boudreau and Nadine
Have a Big Adventure

It isn't very often that I hear from my cousin and his lovely wife; Boudreau and Nadine Gamelle. The reason for this is that they rarely venture very far away from their rural home not far from Sabine, Texas. Boudreau and Nadine live comfortably in the bayou country that borders Texas and Louisiana. I have no idea what they do for a living, but am pretty sure it has something to do with hunting coons, the occasional gator and being a guide to hunters that want to experience life on the bayou. Being Cajun and living in the swamp doesn't mix very well with the urban lifestyle, so when I do hear from Boudreau it signals that he and Nadine have had some wild adventure...an adventure pretty far removed from swamp life.

It appears that this time Boudreau and Nadine went on a Caribbean cruise. Sales of coon and gator must be up this year, or they won some contest from Cajun Clearinghouse. However it happened, their letter is worth sharing. I hope you enjoy their adventure!

Dear Couzin Joe,

Ooowee, Joe we jus' come back from a trip to dat Caribbean and dem islands. Nadine and me we sailed outta Galveston on that big Carnival ship, but I gotta tell ya, I didn't see no carnival barkers or rides any where on dat boat...kinda disappointin'. Holy Moly dats a big boat! Lot bigger dan my flat bottom out in the bayou, don't you know.

They nice people on dat boat too; even if they did make us wear shoes and socks all week. I put a high shine on Nadine's swamp boots for the soirée in the main mess hall each night. And da food was real tasty. Da boys dat served up our meals were from another country so they don't speak so good like Nadine and me. We were a bit disappointed that there were no coon, possum or squirrel on da menu; lot a strange stuff. One night we had strawberry bisque. It was under da soup section on the menu and I was wonderin' if it would be chunks of berries in some hot broth; didn't sound too appetizin', but I sure did like that word bisque...sounds real high tone. I'm thinkin' back in da bayou of servin' up some coon bisque to the city fellers that come a huntin' in the swamp. Any way, when da boys brung us the bisque it was cold. Nadine thought maybe they made a mistake and brought us a smoothie in a bowl. She asked dem boys for a straw, but they found no humor in dat. Me and Nadine played it safe though and got us some shrimp cocktail. We had an appetite for some good old jumbo shrimp, you know the kind dat they serve up down in the parishes on the Loosiana coast. Well they brung us this itsy bitsy bowl with four tiny little shrimp... may a been baby shrimp...I looked at it and said, ooowee, wouldn't take many of them to make a dozen. Them boys left shakin' their heads. Nadine and me pretty much stuck with meat and taters after that.

Lot of water out there in the gulf. Lot bigger than Toledo Bend reservoir. We sailed a couple of days, then the captain parked us in Jamaica. Nice place, real green and wet…kinda like the bayou, only they got some mountains there…no mountains in the swamp. Nadine and me decided to take one of them day long excursions to Margaritaville. They said we would enjoy the seven mile beach and lunch at Margaritaville in Negril. We got us on the bus with a bunch from the boat…about two dozen of us…we thought ooowee two dozen of us and seven miles of beach…we gonna get brown, swim, feast and relax. Guess the brochure missed the part that Margaritaville only got bout 50 yards a dat beach and the part bout the other dozen buses. Joe, we was squeezed in there tighter than red beans and rice in a jar. I knew we was in deep doodoo when Nadine said I best leave her be; she was going off to her special place…sat silent til we got back on the bus. That bus really cheered her up. Why she got even cheerier when we got closer to da boat.

Lots a fun things to do on the boat too. They got entertainment, and gambling and lots of stores right on the boat. There was even two pools. Imagine that, swimming pools on a boat in the middle of all that water. I'm gettin' me a pool for the swamp boat real soon. Found a nice two ringer at the Wal-Mart in Sabine. Me and Nadine wanted to show we had some class (low as it might be) so we went to a few of the art auctions. Seems to me that is sort a reverse bargainin'. Everybody likes a good bargain; can't understand why folks would start out with a low price and try to pay more for those pictures. They did auction off some nice paintin's at low prices. Me and Nadine we bought us one to spruce up the cabin back in the swamp. The auctioneer said it was almost free and that we could have it delivered unframed in a tube or shipped in a frame. Nadine couldn't understand how hangin' that tube on the wall would make the cabin spruce up, so we got us a frame. That almost free artwork now cost us income from two full grown gators. We was committed to havin' a frame instead of a tube so we stuck with it. We should have that artwork before coon season, so you and Jane need to come down to the swamp to see it, the frame, and have some coon bisque.

Captain parked the boat a couple a more times. They have a shopping lady on the boat that tells you where to get all the good bargains on the 'ites'. We had no use for the ites, so we decided we'd jus' look. Me and Nadine aren't sure what all the ites were. There was Tanzanite and Ammalite...I don't know may have been Kryptonite, Dynamite and Silentnite too. And more Diamonds International than McDonald's in Houston, but all in three blocks from the ship. We decided just to people watch... don't see many folks back in the bayou so this is a real treat. Nadine and me hunkered down at this little side-walk café, reminded us of our trip to the French Quarter in N'Awlins, and got us a couple a dem jumbo margaritas. Joe boy that was trouble in a glass. Seems they make those drinks with 150 proof tequila and they don't skimp on it neither. Couple a sips and Nadine couldn't feel her face! Strangest thing happened as we sat there drinkin' and eatin' hot peppered pico de gallo...the shoppin' came to us. Lots a nice folk stopped by our table and we bought all kinds of things without movin' an inch. That Carnival company ought to highlight that shore excursion. We got a bunch a good stuff, but between you and me it was real expensive. Nadine don't know how much we done spent. Didn't want to ruin the good time she was having with the numb face.

Well Joe, we had to go back to the boat and that wasn't easy. Nadine slipped into full body numbness by then. After that it was back to Galveston and on to the swamp. Before I forget, do you want me to send you the coon bisque recipe? Ah heck, you don't trap no coons up in Dallas, do ya? We'll keep a pot simmerin'; maybe put some up and send it to you at the holidays. It'll make a hit with your friends. It was a great sail; we'll do it again some time. Our best to you, Jane and all the Lunchbuckets up your way.

Y'all take care now,
Boudreau

Well folks, there you have it. Sounds like Boudreau and Nadine had a grand time sailing the high seas, and sailing high on the seas. I cannot tell you how many times I have cautioned him and Nadine about over indulging in Tequila. Boudreau and Nadine always seem to have a swell time whenever they go on one of their adventures and his way of recollection is awe inspiring...don't you think. I hope you didn't mind my departure from my usual tales. A letter from Boudreau is just too much to keep to myself.

Until next time best regards,
Joe Lunchbucket

CHAPTER **Thirteen**

WALSTIB

King Arthur and his Knights of the Round Table lived in a magical time and a magical place. Their environment was unlike that of most of the rest of the known world. It was bright, shining and full of adventure. The evils of Modred were outside of their realm, but Arthur and the Knights stood ready to protect their kingdom and their fair maidens. Arthur and the knights shared their lives and fortunes and embarked on the quest for the Holy Grail. The stories of this time are alive and adventuresome. They inspire us to embrace our own quest, fight our own dark knights and chronicle our adventures in search of our own holy grail... whatever that might be.

I have shared with you some of the tales and travels of an aging boomer with the focus on some of the adventures of the Knights of the 8 Corners and have tossed in a few personal stories of the years since my youth. We have fought our own battles with our own Modred. We have pursued and protected our own Guinevere. We have come face to face with the loyalty and betrayal of our own

Lancelot. We have lived life and come through it all with a remarkable youthful zest that still fires us up on a daily basis.

Today we are more high tech in our communications and keeping in touch is an email or 'poke' on Facebook. There are and will be more stories to tell from the past, the present and in the future. Our adventure continues. The souls we have encountered, the memories we have made and the adventures we have pursued this past half century have been and will continue to be our bright and shinning moments...our Camelot.

Rest assured, as long as I am able, I will continue to chronicle the tales and travels of this aging boomer with those stories past, present and future...we cannot yet be done making memories for a later date...and I will rely on those fellow Knights and Ladies of my Round Table to rekindle the tales of our travels together.

I have posted in the bunker from which I spin these stories a quote from an unknown author that needs to be shared, although I am pretty certain that we are living proof of this, philosophy; it reads:

"Life is not a journey to the grave with the intention of arriving safely in a pretty and well preserved body, but rather to skid in broadside, thoroughly used up, totally worn out and loudly proclaiming – WOW...WHAT A RIDE!"

So far it has been quite a ride on all counts and I marvel at what has come my way and it has qualified as WALSTIB...What a long strange trip it's been.

About the author

Joe Lunchbucket grew up in the western suburbs of Chicago, where most of the Chronicles took place. He is confident that the statute of limitations has run out on his minor infractions against the people of Brookfield and the other burbs. Joe attended Southern Illinois University in Carbondale where he received his BS in Economics. He currently lives in Dallas, Texas where he is active in his own Insurance Brokerage firm and writes from the recesses of his reinforced bunker.